THE IMPORTANCE OF

John Steinbeck

by
Tom Ito

Lucent Books, P.O. Box 289011, San Diego, CA 92198-9011

These and other titles are included in The Importance Of biography series:

Alexander the Great	Jim Henson	Jackie Robinson
Napoleon Bonaparte	Thomas Jefferson	Anwar Sadat
Cleopatra	Chief Joseph	Margaret Sanger
Christopher Columbus	Malcolm X	John Steinbeck
Marie Curie	Margaret Mead	Jim Thorpe
Thomas Edison	Michelangelo	Mark Twain
Albert Einstein	Wolfgang Amadeus Mozart	H.G. Wells
Benjamin Franklin	Sir Isaac Newton	
Galileo Galilei	Richard M. Nixon	

Library of Congress Cataloging-in-Publication Data

Ito, Tom
    John Steinbeck / by Tom Ito
        p. cm.—(The Importance of)
    Includes bibliographical references and index.
    ISBN 1-56006-049-2 (alk. paper)
    1. Steinbeck, John, 1902-1968—Biography—Juvenile literature. 2. Novelists, American—20th century—Biography—Juvenile literature. [1. Steinbeck, John, 1902-1968. 2. Authors, American.] I.Title. II. Series.
PS3537.T3234Z71525   1994
813'.52—dc20   92-40923
[B]   CIP
                                                                        AC

Copyright 1994 by Lucent Books, Inc., P.O. Box 289011, San Diego, California, 92198-9011

Printed in the U.S.A.

Contents

Foreword   5
Important Dates in the Life of John Steinbeck   6

INTRODUCTION
Making People Understand Each Other   7

CHAPTER 1
Early Struggles   10

CHAPTER 2
California Camelot   22

CHAPTER 3
Poverty and Persistence   34

CHAPTER 4
An Exalted Endeavor   43

CHAPTER 5
Eventful Years   55

CHAPTER 6
Return to California   64

CHAPTER 7
Turbulent Years   75

CHAPTER 8
In Search of New Challenges   84

CHAPTER 9
The Final Years   92

Notes   102
For Further Reading   105
Additional Works Consulted   107
Index   109
Picture Credits   112
About the Author   112

Foreword

THE IMPORTANCE OF biography series deals with individuals who have made a unique contribution to history. The editors of the series have deliberately chosen to cast a wide net and include people from all fields of endeavor. Individuals from politics, music, art, literature, philosophy, science, sports, and religion are all represented. In addition, the editors did not restrict the series to individuals whose accomplishments have helped change the course of history. Of necessity, this criterion would have eliminated many whose contribution was great, though limited. Charles Darwin, for example, was responsible for radically altering the scientific view of the natural history of the world. His achievements continue to impact the study of science today. Others, such as Chief Joseph of the Nez Percé, played a pivotal role in the history of their own people. While Joseph's influence does not extend much beyond the Nez Percé, his nonviolent resistance to white expansion and his continuing role in protecting his tribe and his homeland remain an inspiration to all.

These biographies are more than factual chronicles. Each volume attempts to emphasize an individual's contributions both in his or her own time and for posterity. For example, the voyages of Christopher Columbus opened the way to European colonization of the New World. Unquestionably, his encounter with the New World brought monumental changes to both Europe and the Americas in his day. Today, however, the broader impact of Columbus's voyages is being critically scrutinized. *Christopher Columbus,* as well as every biography in The Importance Of series, includes and evaluates the most recent scholarship available on each subject.

Each author includes a wide variety of primary and secondary source quotations to document and substantiate his or her work. All quotes are footnoted to show readers exactly how and where biographers derive their information, as well as to provide stepping stones to further research. These quotations enliven the text by giving readers eyewitness views of the life and times of each individual covered in The Importance Of series.

Finally, each volume is enhanced by photographs, bibliographies, chronologies, and comprehensive indexes. For both the casual reader and the student engaged in research, The Importance Of biographies will be a fascinating adventure into the lives of people who have helped shape humanity's past and present, and who will continue to shape its future.

Important Dates in the Life of John Steinbeck

John Steinbeck is born on February 27, in Salinas, California, to John Ernst and Olive Hamilton Steinbeck. — **1902**

1919 — Graduates from Salinas High School; attends Stanford University.

Leaves Stanford without graduating; travels to New York City to pursue a free-lance writing career. — **1925**

1929 — First novel, *Cup of Gold*, is published.

Steinbeck marries Carol Henning. — **1930**

1932 — *The Pastures of Heaven* is published.

To a God Unknown and the first two parts of *The Red Pony* are published. — **1933**

1934 — Steinbeck's mother, Olive Steinbeck, dies; Steinbeck wins O. Henry prize for short story, "The Murderer."

Steinbeck's father, John Ernst Steinbeck, dies; *Tortilla Flat* is published. — **1935**

1936

1937 — *In Dubious Battle* is published.

Of Mice and Men is published and is chosen by the Book-of-the-Month Club. — **1937**

1939 — *The Grapes of Wrath* is published.

1940 — *The Log from "The Sea of Cortez,"* written in collaboration with Ed Ricketts, is published.

Steinbeck wins the Pulitzer Prize for *The Grapes of Wrath*. — **1941**

1942 — Steinbeck is assigned as a correspondent for New York *Herald Tribune* and covers World War II in London, Europe, and North Africa; Steinbeck marries Gwyndolyn Conger.

Steinbeck divorces Carol Henning. — **1943**

Steinbeck's first son, Thom, is born. — **1944**

1945

Steinbeck's second son, John, is born. — **1946** — *Cannery Row* is published.

1947 — *The Pearl* and *The Wayward Bus* are published.

Steinbeck divorces his second wife, Gwyndolyn Conger. — **1948**

1950 — Steinbeck marries Elaine Scott.

East of Eden is published. — **1952**

1961 — Steinbeck's last novel, *The Winter of Our Discontent*, is published.

Travels with Charley is published; Steinbeck receives Nobel Prize for literature. — **1962**

1966 — *America and Americans* is published.

Steinbeck dies on Long Island on December 20. — **1968**

Making People Understand Each Other

In the autumn of 1962, American novelist John Steinbeck was honored with one of the world's highest awards, the Nobel Prize. This presentation capped a distinguished career spanning nearly four decades, during which Steinbeck produced some of the most compelling literature of the twentieth century.

Many of Steinbeck's most memorable novels, including *Of Mice and Men, The Grapes of Wrath*, and *East of Eden*, are esteemed literary classics. They continue to inspire and enlighten new generations of readers with their stirring sagas of human triumph and tragedy. Steinbeck wrote with rugged eloquence and an earthy candor. Many of his books feature impoverished and dispossessed people, such as the American migrant farm workers whose courageous and poignant struggle for survival profoundly moved him. Throughout his life, Steinbeck wrote passionately with what he believed to be a "nervous restlessness, a hunger, a thirst, a yearning for something unknown—perhaps morality."[1] In his most unforgettable stories Stein-

Nobel Prize-winning author John Steinbeck and his wife Elaine celebrate at a reception in his honor. On display are the novels that brought Steinbeck literary fame.

beck wrote of the quest for human fulfillment and dignity in a promised land of opportunity and social equality.

The "Okies"

Steinbeck began his career as a writer during the Great Depression of the 1930s, when millions of people found themselves homeless and unemployed. Poverty swept the entire nation. Steinbeck particularly wanted to write about the thousands of Oklahoma farmers who, desolated by the ruin of their crops and unable to meet their mortgages, found themselves stripped of their lands by the federal government. Derisively dubbed "Okies" by more fortunate farm owners, they resolutely packed their few belongings and began a pilgrimage to the fertile valleys of California in search of work and the promise of renewed prosperity.

The exodus of these courageous people, who Steinbeck saw as born of poverty and sustained by faith, became an enduring inspiration to him and led to the writing of one of his greatest novels: *The Grapes of Wrath* became the number one bestseller in America in 1939 and drew national attention to the plight of the Okies. Here Steinbeck shared with readers his belief in a vision of brotherhood that was a dream of the spirit as well as of the soil. Although the loss of their land had drawn the Okies together in their migration westward, Steinbeck felt that it was the valor they shared as a people that would sustain them in their quest for a new home.

The hardships of the journey to California and the unjust working conditions they encountered in labor camps forced the Okies to unite and support one another in the struggle to survive. This unity, Steinbeck believed, brought dignity to the individual and nobility to the people as a whole. He affirmed his conviction that a brotherhood of simple compassion and courage could return all men to an inheritance of the earth: "My whole work drive," he once wrote, "has been aimed at making people understand each other."[2]

Steinbeck had a great love for America but was often troubled and angered by the social injustices and economic corruption that he saw. Novels such as *In Dubious Battle* related the horrors and brutality of American labor conflicts, and *The Winter of Our Discontent* explored what Steinbeck viewed as the erosion of the American character through a growing obsession with material wealth. In 1959, in a letter to former Illinois governor and presidential candidate Adlai Stevenson, Steinbeck related his thoughts on national greed.

Adlai do you remember two kinds of Christmases? There is one kind in a house where there is little and a present represents not only love but sacrifice. . . . Then there is the other kind of Christmas with presents piled high, the gifts of guilty parents as bribes because they have nothing else to give.

Well, it seems to me that America now is like the second kind of Christmas. Having too many THINGS they spend their hours and money on the couch searching for a soul. A strange species we are. We can stand anything God and Nature can throw at us save only plenty. If I wanted to destroy a nation, I would give it too much and I would have it on its knees, miserable, greedy and sick.[3]

One of Steinbeck's most famous novels, The Grapes of Wrath, *was inspired by the "Okies" and their courageous westward migration during the Great Depression.*

Steinbeck saw and wrote about what he believed was the dark side of the American dream. He saw in America's freedom the source of a prosperous national economy but was outraged at the poverty endured by many citizens. Steinbeck believed it obscene that in a land describing itself as a democracy, farmers could be deprived of their lands, migrant workers victimized by organized thugs, and children barred from attending public schools because of their color and race. As a writer, Steinbeck felt driven to look upon and record what he found to be both admirable and shameful in our national character and to attempt through his work to raise public consciousness and urge social reform.

In his Nobel Prize acceptance speech, Steinbeck eloquently expressed his convictions and ethics as a writer:

The ancient commission of the writer has not changed. He is charged with exposing our many grievous faults and failures, with dredging up to the light our dark and dangerous dreams for the purpose of improvement.

Furthermore, the writer is delegated to declare and to celebrate man's proven capacity for greatness of heart and spirit—for gallantry in defeat—for courage, compassion and love. In the endless war against weakness and despair, these are the bright rally-flags of hope and of emulation.

I hold that a writer who does not passionately believe in the perfectibility of man, has no dedication nor any membership in literature.[4]

John Steinbeck's life was a testament to these principles. Although in the end he was not fully satisfied with any of his published works, his lifelong exemplification of the ideal of "perfectibility" has earned him an enduring place in literature.

1 Early Struggles

John Ernst Steinbeck Jr. was born in Salinas, California, on February 27, 1902. He was the only son and the third child of John Ernst Steinbeck and Olive Hamilton Steinbeck, who also had three daughters, Elizabeth, Esther, and Mary.

As a child, Steinbeck was captivated by the rolling hills of the rural Salinas Valley. A love for his homeland remained with Steinbeck throughout his life.

At the time of Steinbeck's birth, California was still in many regions an undeveloped frontier. After a half-century of statehood, exciting memories remained of the great stampede for gold fifty years earlier, and the very name of California continued to beckon people westward as a land promising fortune and wealth.

Steinbeck cherished a love for the land of his birth that would remain with him throughout his life. As an imaginative child, he had looked upon the Gabilan Mountains, which rise above the Salinas Valley, as a protective and sheltering range. In the autobiographical introduction to his novel *East of Eden*, he remembers them as "light gay mountains full of sun and loveliness and a kind of invitation, so that you wanted to climb into their warm foothills almost as you want to climb into the lap of a beloved mother."[5]

The Salinas Valley of Steinbeck's childhood was primarily rural and agricultural. Vast acres of farm fields raising such crops as lettuce and sugar beets dominated the long fertile plain that stretched between the ranges of the Santa Lucia and Gabilan Mountains. As a restless and imaginative boy, Steinbeck spent much of his time wandering through the wooded hills, finding adventure in solemn daydreams and in the small discoveries of the secret, intimate kingdoms of nature and wildlife for which he was to develop a lifelong fascination. He would later wistfully relate to readers this youthful enchantment with earthy solitude:

> I remember my childhood names for grasses and secret flowers. I remember where a toad may live and what time the birds awaken in the summer—and what trees and seasons smelled like.[6]

The mountains offered a sanctuary of romantic escape for the boy. Below and beyond them stretched the great valley of his home and his family. The farming people laboring in the fields were neighbors and friends. In later years Steinbeck would draw from their lives much of the inspiration for the vivid and moving narratives of his books.

Parental Conflicts

The Steinbeck family owned a modest but comfortable Victorian house in Salinas. The elder John Steinbeck was an accountant who had begun working for the Southern Pacific Milling Company in King City and later moved to Salinas to manage the Sperry Flour Mill. When economic difficulties forced his dismissal at the mill, Steinbeck's father decided to go into business for himself by opening a feed and grain store.

The enterprise struggled to survive but eventually failed. A close friend secured for Steinbeck's father a position as an accountant for the Spreckles Sugar Company. Although he functioned in this position with efficiency, the loss of his own business was a bitter blow to the elder

While their mother looks on, John and his sister Mary pose playfully for the camera in front of the family's Victorian home.

Steinbeck. Steinbeck remembered his father as being a gentle, conventional, and quietly desperate man:

> I remember his restlessness. It sometimes filled the house to a howling although he did not speak often. He was a singularly silent man—first I suppose because he had few words and second because he had no one to say them to. He was strong rather than profound. . . . I often wonder about him. In my struggle to be a writer, it was he who supported and backed me and explained me—not my mother. She wanted me desperately to be something decent like a banker. She would have liked me to be a successful writer like Tarkington, but this she didn't believe I could do. But my father wanted me to be myself. Isn't that odd. He ad-

mired anyone who laid down his line and followed it undeflected to the end. I think this was because he abandoned his star in little duties and responsibility. To be anything pure requires an arrogance he did not have, and a selfishness he could not bring himself to assume. He was a man intensely disappointed in himself. And I think he liked the complete ruthlessness of my design to be a writer in spite of mother and hell.[7]

In later years, Steinbeck frequently wrote of the moral support he received from his father while he was becoming a writer. Although he loved his mother, Steinbeck never shared the close affection for her that he did with his father. Her apparent lack of faith in his ability to succeed as a writer wounded his sense of self-esteem, and he would remember this throughout his life. Yet much of Steinbeck's creative and fanciful perception of the world was greatly influenced by his mother's own imaginative nature. In his biography of Steinbeck, Jackson J. Benson asserts that it was Olive Steinbeck who urged her son to open his mind to the subtle wonders of life:

> It was she who planted the seed with her bedroom stories of enchanted forests, she who encouraged her son to use his imagination, to discover a world made up of both the seen and the unseen, and to perceive the nature of things intuitively and poetically, and not only by the common sense that alone was valued in the masculine society of a "frontier town."[8]

A Love of Literature Is Born

Both parents encouraged their children to read aloud as a way of providing family entertainment for themselves and others. The discipline of the lessons was at first re-

John's love of literature was fostered by his parents, John and Olive Steinbeck, who encouraged their children to read aloud for entertainment.

The Secret Book

Steinbeck's belief that literature should be a testament to man's gallantry was inspired in childhood when he read Thomas Malory's book Morte d'Arthur. *Steinbeck recalled his love for what he called his "secret book" in the introduction of his own novel,* The Acts of King Arthur and His Noble Knights.

"And in that scene were all the vices that ever were—and courage and sadness and frustration, but particularly gallantry—perhaps the only single quality of man that the West has invented. I think my sense of right and wrong, my feeling of noblesse oblige [nobility obliges] and any thought I may have against the oppressor and for the oppressed, came from this secret book. . . .

I was not frightened to find that there were evil knights, as well as noble ones. In my town [Salinas] there were men who wore the clothes of virtue whom I knew to be bad. In pain or sorrow or confusion, I went back to my magic book. Children are violent and cruel—and good— and I was all of these—and all of these were in the secret book. If I could not choose my way at the crossroads of love and loyalty, neither could Lancelot. I could understand the darkness of Mordred because he is in me too; and there was some Galahad in me, but perhaps not enough. The Grail feeling was there, however, deep-planted, and perhaps always will be."

sisted by their son but then eventually accepted by him with growing enthusiasm. For his ninth birthday, Steinbeck was given a copy of Sir Thomas Malory's *Morte d'Arthur*. It was the first book Steinbeck owned and he later recalled the great influence of this gift on his life:

> One day, an aunt gave me a book and fatuously ignored my resentment. I stared at the black print with hatred, and then gradually the pages opened and let me in. The magic happened. The Bible and Shakespeare and *Pilgrim's Progress* belonged to everyone. But this was mine—secretly mine. It was a cut version of . . . *Morte d'Arthur* of Thomas Malory. I loved the old spelling of the words—and the words no longer used. Perhaps a passionate love for the English language opened to me from this one book.[9]

As a student at Salinas High School, Steinbeck excelled in English and later served as editor of the school yearbook, *El Gabilan,* in which his first published work appeared. He was fascinated by words and their power to achieve a perfect expression of ideas. By the time Steinbeck completed his freshman year in high school, he had decided to become a writer.

Steinbeck (top row, far left) poses with the Salinas High track team for a yearbook photo. In high school Steinbeck excelled in English, and served as editor of the school yearbook.

The College Rebel

Steinbeck was accepted to Stanford University as an English major and began attending classes in the fall of 1919. To pay his way through college, Steinbeck found it necessary to attend classes half the year and work at various odd jobs the other half. His intermittent career as a university student proved to be a series of dismal disappointments. Steinbeck was an intensely shy youth, and he felt awkward and uncomfortable at the few collegiate social events he attended. He entirely avoided the fraternity and sorority circles, which he believed to be snobbish. Although Steinbeck eventually formed fast friendships with a few select individuals on campus, he generally preferred to spend the time apart from his studies writing in solitude. During his years at Stanford, Steinbeck preferred to view himself as a writer in training rather than

as a college student. He believed that writers should be free thinkers and enjoyed casting himself as a rebel and social outcast.

"I think rebellion man's highest state," Steinbeck declared in a letter to his friend Carl Wilhelmson during one quarter break. "All that we regard most highly in art, literature, government, philosophy, or even those changes which are the result of anatomic evolution had their beginnings in rebellion in an individual."[10] Despite such defiant declarations, however, Steinbeck did attract various comrades who, like himself, nourished artistic or literary ambitions. Steinbeck led these friends in rowdy campus pranks and boisterous drinking sessions.

The routine of college life generally grated on Steinbeck's restless nature. He identified more with colorful and exciting literary figures like Jack London, who had written from his own experiences as a sailor in the Pacific and a gold miner in the Klondike. Steinbeck had read these books as a boy and longed to embark on similar adventures.

Steinbeck had applied to Stanford primarily to please his parents, who believed that a college education would ensure a successful and secure future for their son. Once he had enrolled, however, Steinbeck proceeded to select (whenever his counselor permitted) only the courses that interested him or that he felt would prepare him for a career in writing. For the next six years, he struggled through an erratic course of study that ended with him leaving Stanford altogether in the spring of 1925. He never made another attempt to achieve a college degree.

One exceptional and positive event occurred during Steinbeck's studies at Stanford, however. He took a course in short story writing under a gifted and strict professor named Edith Ronald Mirrielees.

Professor Mirrielees had stressed professional discipline as essential to the craft of fine writing. Under her stern instruction, Steinbeck strove to develop a "lean, terse style" in his work.[11]

Mirrielees often required Steinbeck to revise his assignments heavily, to eliminate excessive ornamentation in his writing. At first Steinbeck found this discipline difficult to accept. He loved words and viewed writing both as a means of expressing his thoughts and feelings and as an opportunity to exercise his vocabulary. He eventually, however, came to appreciate Professor Mirrielees's insistence on conciseness and to acknowledge how such discipline in style clarified his writing. "She does one thing for you," Steinbeck admitted in a letter to his friend Robert Cathcart. "She makes you get over what you want to say."[12]

Although he had decided to leave college and was determined to pursue a full-

A Creed for Excellent Writing

Professor Edith Ronald Mirrielees exerted a great influence over Steinbeck's studies at Stanford. In The True Adventures of John Steinbeck, Writer, *Jackson J. Benson discusses this influence.*

"[Steinbeck's friend] Webster Street, who took Mirrielees's short-story-writing class during the same period that Steinbeck was working with her, recalls that she had three basic tenets. The first was to ask yourself, after having written a story, whether or not you had accomplished what you set out to do. The second was to ask, Is it convincing to the reader? And the third, was the fabric she was thinking of as the sense of 'truth.' It may not be true in a universal sense, but it may be true in relation to the fabric of the story. In her teaching, there was a great emphasis on a common sense approach, on clear logic, and on the questions of what is believable and why."

Steinbeck (front row, tenth from left) at the Stanford Frosh-Senior "Tie-Up," in 1919. The routine of college life never agreed with Steinbeck, who left Stanford, after six years of study, without a degree.

time writing career, Steinbeck was far from confident about his future. He knew that his parents were disappointed at his failure to obtain a degree at Stanford. Many of his former classmates had already graduated and embarked on promising careers. Steinbeck seemed the least likely of his classmates to succeed.

Hope and Failure in New York

Packing his typewriter, a few clothes, and a bundle of short stories he hoped to publish, Steinbeck headed for a mountain resort at Lake Tahoe in June 1925, where a friend had secured him a job. He planned to earn enough money to travel to New York City and pursue a career as a freelance writer. Steinbeck worked at Lake Tahoe throughout the summer as a maintenance man. In November 1925 he signed on to a working berth of a freighter bound for New York. The sea voyage included passage through the jungle waters of the Panama Canal, and this part of the adventure experience proved to be the most enjoyable. Traveling through the Caribbean, he explored Panama City and the streets of Havana. The tropical region made a vivid impression on Steinbeck, and he used the exotic area as the setting for his first novel, *Cup of Gold*.

When Steinbeck arrived in New York City, his meager funds nearly depleted, he found work as a construction laborer hauling cement in wheelbarrows. A few months later an uncle of Steinbeck's arrived in the city and secured a job for him as a newspaper cub reporter on the *New York American*. Steinbeck soon learned that he was sometimes expected to resort to unscrupulous methods to obtain material for his articles. He later recalled his first experience in newspaper journalism as bewildering and frustrating.

They gave me stories to cover in Queens and Brooklyn [outer boroughs of New York City] and I would get lost and spend hours trying to find my way back [to Manhattan]. I couldn't learn to steal a picture from a desk when a bereaved family refused to be photographed, and I invariably got emotionally involved and tried to kill the whole story in order to save the subject.[13]

After several weeks at the *New York American*, Steinbeck realized that he was not suited for the work. Because he lacked experience, the editors assigned him stories that were generally unimportant events with little news value. The structure and boundaries of newswriting held no appeal for Steinbeck, who preferred a more liberal, creative style. He had little enthusiasm for his reporting job, and this indifference became apparent to his editors. He frequently failed to show up for work and was fired.

Steinbeck was at first relieved over his termination from the *New York American*. He was confident that he could earn his living as a free-lance writer and began sending some of his stories to magazines. By the spring of 1926, Steinbeck had run out of money and was desperate. He had neither obtained employment as a writer nor sold any of his stories. In addition, Steinbeck had fallen behind in the rent of his one-room Manhattan apartment and often found it necessary to go without meals.

During this grim time, one opportunity brightened Steinbeck's prospects. A former college classmate, Amasa "Ted" Miller, introduced Steinbeck to Guy Holt, an editor at the publishing house of Robert McBride & Company. Holt read some of

A Young Writer's Philosophy

As a young man, Steinbeck developed a lifelong habit of sharing thoughts about writing with friends. This excerpt from one of Steinbeck's letters included in Jackson J. Benson's biography, relates some advice to hopeful playwright Bob Cathcart in 1929.

"Like a great number of young writers (me for instance) you are very much, almost too much interested in paradox, aren't you? When analysed, paradox holds water with difficulty as a theme literaturesque, and yet the bulk of modern writing grabs it and will not let it go. It has the same hold on modern writing that coincidence did on that of the period just finished. Eventually you will come to the conclusion that there is no such thing as metaphysics, that paradox is a manner rather than an effect. It doesn't make much difference anyway. The main thing just now with all of us is to get just as many words on paper as possible and then to destroy the paper."

In New York City Steinbeck worked as a reporter for the New York American. *His dislike for the job strengthened his resolve to succeed as a free-lance writer.*

Steinbeck's short stories and encouraged the young author to submit a refined collection to McBride for publication.

Steinbeck worked on the short story manuscript in a fever of excitement, but he found upon delivering it that Holt had left McBride for another publishing company, John Day & Company. The editor who had replaced Holt informed Steinbeck that McBride had revised its policy and had no immediate plans to publish a collection of short stories. Although disappointed, Steinbeck persisted and carried his work to John Day & Company, only to be informed that they did not publish fiction submitted by unknown writers.

Steinbeck was devastated. His immediate prospects for being published ended with the second rejection. In desperation and near starvation, he tried to go back to

being a manual laborer, to earn enough money to survive. "But by that time short feeding had taken hold," Steinbeck later recalled:

> I could hardly lift a pick. I had trouble climbing the six flights [of stairs] back to my room. My friend loaned me a dollar and I bought two loaves of rye bread and a bag of dried herrings and never left my room for a week. I was afraid to go out on the street—actually afraid of traffic—the noise. Afraid of the landlord and afraid of people. Afraid even of acquaintances.[14]

In this state of exhaustion, Steinbeck decided to leave New York. Amasa Miller was able to find Steinbeck a job as a waiter aboard a ship bound for California, where he could work for his passage. Packing his few belongings and rejected manuscripts, Steinbeck boarded the ship and headed for home.

First Winter of Discontent

Once in California, Steinbeck returned to Lake Tahoe where he obtained a job as the caretaker for a large estate at the lake and was allowed to live in a small cabin. Winter descended and Steinbeck was snowed in for eight months. In the imposed solitude of the Sierra Nevada, Steinbeck was forced to grapple with his own loneliness and personal sense of isolation. Sitting alone in a tiny cabin surrounded by a frozen wilderness, he felt entirely cut off from the rest of the world.

Steinbeck's writing offered the only refuge in this bleak existence. He turned to the task of writing a fictionalized biography of the pirate Henry Morgan. The manuscript (ms) he produced that winter would become his first novel, *Cup of Gold*. Two days before his twenty-sixth birthday, Steinbeck wrote his close friend Carlton Sheffield a letter in which he revealed many of the self-doubts and personal regrets that haunted him at the time:

> I am finishing the Henry [Morgan] ms [*Cup of Gold*], out of duty, but I have no hope of it anymore. I shall probably pack it in Limbo balls and place it among the lost hopes in the chest of

A Confession of Fear

Steinbeck wrote his first novel, Cup of Gold, *in a cabin near Lake Tahoe. The experience provided him with a testing ground in dealing with solitude and personal isolation. Included in* Steinbeck: A Life in Letters *is this letter in which Steinbeck confides to his friend Webster Street his deep sense of loneliness.*

"Do you know, one of the things that made me come here, was, as you guessed, that I am frightfully afraid of being alone. The fear of the dark is only part of it. I wanted to break that fear in the middle, because I am afraid much of my existence is going to be more or less alone, and I might as well go into training for it. It comes on me at night mostly, in little waves of panic, that constrict something in my stomach. But don't you think it is good to fight these things? Last night, some quite large animal came and sniffed under the door. I presume it was a coyote, though I do not know. The moon had not come up, and when I ran outside there was nothing to be seen. But the main thing was that I was frightened, even though I knew it could be nothing but a coyote. Don't tell any one I am afraid. I do not like to be suspected of being afraid."

the years. Good bye, Henry. I thought you were heroic but you are only, as was said of you, a babbler of words and rather clumsy about it.

I shall make an elegy to Henry Morgan, who is a monument to my own lack of ability. I shall go ahead, but I wonder if that sharp agony of words will occur to me again. I wonder if I shall ever be drunken with rhythms anymore. I am twenty-six and I am not young any more. I shall write good novels but hereafter I ride Pegasus with a saddle and martingale [device for restraining a horse's movement], for I am afraid Pegasus will rear and kick, and I am not the sure steady horseman I once was.[15]

In late January 1929, Steinbeck received a startling communication from Amasa Miller. Nearly four years had passed since Miller had offered to try to place his friend's manuscripts with a publisher. True to his word, however, Miller had persisted and now wired Steinbeck the announcement that McBride and Company would publish *Cup of Gold*.

The little novel appeared on bookstore shelves in the autumn of 1929, and its limited edition of 1,500 sold fairly well, especially during the Christmas season. Publication of his novel renewed Steinbeck's self-confidence. In a letter written to former classmate Grove A. Day in December 1929, he gave an optimistic and humorous estimate of his achievement

Steinbeck blossomed in the imposed solitude of Lake Tahoe. During his two year stay, he completed his first book and gained a greater sense of self-confidence.

A Time of Personal Growth

During the years spent writing at Lake Tahoe, Steinbeck was able to accomplish the writing of his first book and also gained a greater sense of self-confidence. One of the letters in Steinbeck: A Life in Letters *from December 1929 to former Stanford classmate Grove A. Day, recalls the maturing influence of this period.*

"I don't care any more of what people think of me. I'll tell you how it happened. You will remember at Stanford that I went about being different characters. I even developed a theory that one had no personality in essence, that one was a reflection of a mood plus the moods of other persons present. I wasn't pretending to be something I wasn't. For the moment I was truly the person I thought I was.

Well, I went into the mountains and stayed two years. I was snowed in eight months of the year and saw no one except my two Airedales. There were millions of fir trees and the snow was deep and it was very quiet. You can't have a show with no audience. Gradually, all the poses slipped off and when I came out of the hills I didn't have any poses any more. It was rather sad, but far less trouble. I am happier than I have ever been in my life."

and professional prospects, indicating that he had resolved some of his earlier misgivings and doubts:

Long ago I determined that anyone who appraised The Cup of Gold for what it was should be entitled to a big kiss. The book was an immature experiment written for the purpose of getting all the wisecracks (known by sophomores as epigrams) and all the autobiographical material (which hounds us until we get it said) out of my system. And I really did not intend to publish it. The book accomplished its purgative purpose. I am no more concerned with myself very much. I can write about other people.—The new book is a straightforward and simple attempt to set down some characters in a situation and nothing else. If there is any beauty in it, it is a beauty of idea. I seem to have outgrown [James Branch] Cabell [a favorite contemporary writer of Steinbeck's]. The new method is far the more difficult of the two. It reduces a single idea to a single sentence and does not allow one to write a whole chapter with it as Cabell does. I think I shall write some very good books indeed.[16]

Those words were to prove prophetic. The decade of the 1930s loomed a few days away. During that period, Steinbeck produced some of his most memorable works and refined his talents into a powerful, passionate literary style.

2 California Camelot

Steinbeck's return to California in 1929 marked the beginning of a period in the writer's life that would bring both professional challenges and personal happiness. The natural beauty of Lake Tahoe was a welcome change from the congested environment of New York City, which Steinbeck had found so oppressive. California was to be Steinbeck's home for the next twelve years, and the coastal and agricultural regions near Salinas, his birthplace, would provide the settings for some of his most memorable books.

While in the midst of composing *Cup of Gold* in Lake Tahoe, Steinbeck had met and fallen in love with Carol Henning, a vacationing secretary from San Jose, California. The couple was married in January 1930 and moved into a modest rented house in Los Angeles County. Once they had settled into their new home, Steinbeck ambitiously continued his writing. He was involved at this time with two books. The first was a manuscript he had begun several months earlier titled *To an Unknown God*. The second book was a novella, *Dissonant Symphony*.

Encouraged by Carol's confidence in his talent, Steinbeck found a happiness in marriage that appeared to harmonize with his writing endeavors. Shortly after the wedding he wrote a letter to former Stanford classmate Carl Wilhelmson, expressing this contentment:

> Carol is a good influence on my work. I am putting five hours every day on the rewriting of this one *[To an Unknown God]* and in the evenings I have started another *[Dissonant Symphony]*. I

While in Lake Tahoe, Steinbeck met and fell in love with Carol Henning. The couple was married in 1930.

A Young Author's Restlessness

Learning that his first novel Cup of Gold *was to be published left Steinbeck with mixed feelings of elation and dismay. This excerpt from a letter to Amasa Miller, found in Jackson J. Benson's* The True Adventures of John Steinbeck, Writer, *indicates Steinbeck's strong restlessness over not yet having begun work on another manuscript.*

"I have been gloating and sorrowing in my freedom. It seemed good to be without the curse of a literary fetus and at the same time I have had a feeling of lostness, much I imagine, like that felt by an old soldier when he has been discharged from the army and has no one to tell him what time to brush his teeth. Bad as novels are, they do regulate our lives and give us a responsibility. While this book *[Cup of Gold]* was being written I felt that I was responsible for someone. If I stopped, the characters died. But now it is finished and the words of it are spelled correctly and the punctuation is sitting about in proper places and most of the foolishness has been left on other sheets with blue marks through it. And I am beginning to hate it entirely because I never wrote anything in my life that was spelled correctly. I use punctuation marks to keep my hands busy while my brain is keeping up with my chirography. And, so I shall be embarking on a new piece of work very soon."

have the time and the energy and it gives me pleasure to work, and now I do not seem to have to fight as much reluctance to work as I used to have. The start comes much easier. The new book is just a series of short stories or sketches loosely and foolishly tied together. There are a number of little things I have wanted to write for a long time, some of them ridiculous and some of them more serious, and so I am putting them in a ridiculous fabric.[17]

Very little is known about the material in *Dissonant Symphony*. Steinbeck's attempt to complete this book proved to be a frus-

trating disappointment. After spending several months in a vain effort to develop a satisfactory plot for the novella, Steinbeck discarded the manuscript and the book was never published. The writing of *To an Unknown God* proved to be a more successful endeavor, and Steinbeck continued to work on the book intermittently until its publication in 1933.

By August 1930 the Steinbecks' meager finances were so depleted that the couple decided to return to Pacific Grove and live in a cottage owned by Steinbeck's father. In October 1930 Steinbeck met a young marine biologist named Edward Ricketts. Their first encounter, in the waiting room of a dentist's office in Monterey, made a singular impression on Steinbeck. The writer, in agony over an aching tooth, was astonished to see a young man enter the office carrying a large, freshly extracted molar. Ricketts had grown impatient waiting for the dentist's attention and had performed the extraction himself.

The incident was typical of the unconventional Ricketts. A native of Chicago, Ricketts had grown up in that city and worked his way through the University of Chicago to earn a bachelor of science degree. In 1923 Ricketts owned a biological

Ed Ricketts became Steinbeck's lifelong friend and mentor. He served as a model for Cannery Row's *Doc, one of Steinbeck's most famous characters.*

supply house in Monterey called Pacific Laboratories, Inc. The laboratory provided a number of high schools and colleges with various animal and sea life specimens for biological study.

The laboratory doubled as Ricketts's home. It was located in a district known as Cannery Row because of a nearby sardine cannery. A slender, unassuming man of quiet charisma, Ricketts became a popular resident of Cannery Row who received numerous visitors at his laboratory. The collection of animals and ocean life specimens in Ricketts's laboratory were a great attraction to the many neighborhood children, and adults found Ed to be an entertaining conversationalist. Ricketts was to become Steinbeck's closest friend and mentor. The two men shared a fascination for natural history, particularly marine biology.

Ricketts became the model for a number of characters in several of Steinbeck's books and is best remembered as the inspiration for Doc, in the novel *Cannery Row*. The eighteen-year friendship with Ricketts profoundly influenced Steinbeck.

A Lifelong Professional Alliance Begins

Spurred on by the encouragement and literary criticism of both his wife and Ed Ricketts, Steinbeck strove to advance his writing career with a growing assertiveness. In the spring of 1931, the young author began a professional association with the literary agency of Mavis McIntosh and Elizabeth Otis, which was to endure throughout his career. Steinbeck was immediately impressed by the two agents'

An Author's Modest Appraisal

Despite his great passion for writing, Steinbeck often had ambivalent feelings about being an author. One of the letters included in Steinbeck: A Life in Letters *contains these words to George Albee, expressing Steinbeck's early diffidence.*

"I don't know why the publication of a book should impress you. I've met a number of people who publish books and judging from most of them, the fact of publication seems to make a horse's ass of a man. So forget about it. I've never heard of a book that made any money and I have no desire to speak before women's clubs. Waiting for these contracts has stopped my work a little, that's all. And you must remember that the moment Mr. Ballou [Steinbeck's editor for *The Pastures of Heaven*] buys a book it's his property and he has to think it wonderful or he can't sell it. That's the first principle of salesmanship: believe in your product no matter how rotten it is."

supportive encouragement of his work, which he described in a letter to a fellow writer, George Albee, shortly after signing with the firm, McIntosh & Otis:

> This week I had a letter from Mavis McIntosh, and, if I had not known her method of doing business, I should be very suspicious of her boundless enthusiasm for my mss [manuscripts]. However I am fond of anyone who can raise my spirits as she has raised mine. And the personal interest evinced makes me think she will actually try to find a publisher for me. Also I will not be cut off from communication any more for she will let me know whether anything has happened. Have you sent mss. to her, too? I hope you have. Carl Wilhelmson recommended me and Carl is one of her especial pets. I am rewriting one more short story to send

out and then I shall go back to *The Pastures of Heaven.*[18]

The Pastures of Heaven, composed as a series of short stories and published in 1932, revealed a considerable improvement in narrative style over *Cup of Gold*. Steinbeck was elated over the apparent enthusiasm with which his publisher received the book. In a letter written to George Albee in March 1932, Steinbeck revealed his excitement and pride over the sale of his second book:

> The *Pastures* have been curiously fortunate. [The publishing house] Cape and Smith accepted it with some enthusiasm within three days of its submission to them. According to M&O [McIntosh & Otis] they showed a nice enthusiasm and intend to feature it on their fall list. I am very glad, more for my folks' sake than for my own. They

love it so much. Dad's shoulders are straighter for it and mother beams. I am no longer a white elephant, you see. I am justified in the eyes of their neighbors. It was nice of Miss O. [Elizabeth Otis] to wire. If this firm will only allow me a dedication to my parents, they will be extremely happy.[19]

In the spring of 1932, Cape and Smith was reorganized into a new firm, Jonathan Cape and Robert Ballou, Inc. Robert Ballou, a former literary editor of the *Chicago Daily News*, had read Steinbeck's manuscript with great enthusiasm. Steinbeck's excitement over the publication of *The*

Pastures of Heaven turned to disappointment, however, when the book failed to sell well. His new publisher had suffered numerous business reverses as a result of the Great Depression. Because of these financial difficulties, the company was unable to advertise the book upon its release or to provide it with wide distribution.

During this period, Steinbeck had also continued to refine the writing of his novel *To an Unknown God*. After several changes, the book had evolved into a novelized historical saga of the Salinas Valley. The book became a labor of love to Steinbeck, who felt a deep affection for that fertile agricultural region of central Cali-

Steinbeck's beloved Salinas Valley provided the setting for To a God Unknown, *a novel that illustrates the spiritual and physical bond between man and nature.*

fornia that he regarded as his homeland. "As a matter of fact," Steinbeck had confided in a letter written to Amasa Miller in the summer of 1930, "I am very much emotionally tied up with the whole place. It has a soul which is lacking in the east."[20]

Although Steinbeck had not yet outgrown his overuse of florid symbolism, the book contains some fine writing on nature in passages that are often moving and powerful in their intensity of emotion and beauty of expression. The book was published in 1933 by Jonathan Cape and Robert Ballou under the title, *To a God Unknown.* Many Steinbeck readers consider it to be a forerunner in theme and setting to his later epic, *East of Eden.*

To a God Unknown is a somewhat mystical tale of a family patriarch named Joseph Wayne and his compelling devotion to the farmland he acquires in a California valley. In this book Steinbeck expressed his conviction that man and every other living element of nature are interrelated. This spiritual and physical bond was illustrated in Steinbeck's description of Joseph Wayne's passionate attachment to his land.

Despite the enthusiasm of Steinbeck's agents, *To a God Unknown* proved to be a poor seller, and financial difficulties continued to plague Steinbeck. Although his books had not yet achieved commercial success, (Mavis) McIntosh and (Elizabeth) Otis continued to have great faith in Steinbeck's talent and encouraged him to persist with his writing.

"The Red Pony"

Although Steinbeck was discouraged over the difficulty of finding a publisher for his books, his love of literature led him to

---

A Creative Partnership

Many of Steinbeck's early novels were typed and edited by his first wife, Carol. Steinbeck's appreciation of her diligent assistance was expressed in this letter to George Albee, which is included in Steinbeck: A Life in Letters.

"Yesterday I went collecting with Ed [Ricketts]. The first time I had been out in a long time. It is fine spring now and I enjoyed it a lot. Went over to Santa Cruz. Carol wouldn't go because she was typing and wouldn't take the time off. It would have done her good. But we're broke now and one hamburger was all we could afford. I had been working longer than she had so I took the day off. Today back at revising and proofreading. I'm making dumplings for dinner. I hope they're good. It's a dirty shame Carol has to work so hard. She's putting in nine hours a day at it. I wish I could do it but my typing is so very lousy."

Carol's Cottage Industry

To supplement the couple's meager income, Carol Steinbeck decided to form her own advertising company with a friend. In a letter to Amasa Miller, included in Benson's biography, Steinbeck related an affectionately humorous account of the progress of Carol's enterprise.

"Carol and another girl have just opened [an advertising agency] in Monterey. They have a number of accounts, no competitors on the [Monterey] peninsula, and they seem to be raising hell with business proceedings on the peninsula. And, to refute the inevitable anti-feminist propaganda, I am nominally the head of the firm. But I don't know a thing about advertising although now and then I do have a little idea they can use. . . . Both of them have had extensive experience in both advertising and publicity. Their most amusing account is with a local poetess. $10 a month retainer—heavy space rates for publicity stories and 25 percent of any increased sales in the lady's four volumes of poetry. I think that is sufficiently amusing. A pair of cutthroats they are."

---

attempt numerous other forms of writing. Steinbeck's short stories during this period included a series called "The Red Pony." The first two stories of this series appeared in the *North American Review* in 1933. "The Red Pony" relates the story of a young boy named Jody and his rise to maturity upon the death of his beloved horse. Many of the incidents detailed in stories of "The Red Pony" were drawn from Steinbeck's recollections of his own childhood.

Steinbeck produced a variety of writing during this period that allowed him to experiment with various literary forms and to test his creative versatility. Although Steinbeck was still plagued by poverty, his writing was progressing well. Carol Steinbeck continued to encourage him and worked alongside her husband, typing his manuscripts. A letter written to George Albee from Salinas, in 1933, reveals the close collaboration between the author and his wife:

The pony story is finally finished and the second draft done. I don't know when Carol will find time to type it, but when she does, I'll send the second draft and then you won't have to bother to send it back. It is an unpretentious story. I think the philosophic content is so buried that it will not bother anybody. Carol likes it, but I am afraid our minds are somewhat grown together so that we see with the same eyes and feel with the same emotions. You can see whether you like it at all. There never was more than a half hour of uninterrupted work put on it. . . . I don't see how it can have much continuity, but Carol says it has some.[21]

Following publication of the first two stories of "The Red Pony" in the *North American Review*, Steinbeck wrote additional stories for the series. The entire collection was published in 1937 as a novel titled *The Red Pony*.

The early years of the Great Depression spent in Pacific Grove were for the most part a happy period in the writer's life. Despite their financial distress, the Steinbecks and a circle of friends, including Ed Ricketts, formed a supportive society that encouraged one another's artistic and occupational endeavors. Years later in an article written for *Esquire*, Steinbeck recalled his early struggles with nostalgia:

> The Depression was no financial shock to me. I didn't have any money to lose, but in common with millions I did dislike hunger and cold. I had two assets. My father owned a tiny three-room cottage in Pacific Grove in California, and he let me live in it without rent. That was the first safety. Pacific Grove is on the sea. That was the second. People in inland cities or in the closed and shuttered industrial cemeteries had greater problems than I. Given the sea a man must be very stupid to starve. The great reservoir of food is always available. I took a large part of my protein food from the ocean.
>
> I must drop the "I" for "we" now, for there was a fairly large group of us poor kids, all living alike. We pooled our troubles, our money when we had some, our inventiveness, and our pleasures. I remember it as a warm and friendly time. Only illness frightened us.[22]

Soon illness and death were to cast the shadow of tragedy over the Steinbeck fam-

Hundreds wait in line at a soup kitchen during the Great Depression. Despite financial distress, the early depression years were a happy period in Steinbeck's life.

ily. Early in 1933, Olive Steinbeck was stricken by paralysis, which left her a helpless invalid. Steinbeck and Carol spent much of their time living alternately in their Pacific Grove cottage and in the family house in Salinas, where they made their best attempt to care for Olive. The elder Steinbeck was devastated with grief, and his son revealed the alarm and sorrow he felt over the agonized suffering of his parents in a letter to his former publisher, Robert Ballou:

> My father collapsed a week ago under the six months' strain and very nearly landed in the same position as my mother. It was very close.

He [Steinbeck's father] is like an engine that isn't moored tightly and that just shakes itself to pieces. His nerves are gone and that has brought on numbness and loss of eyesight and he worries [about] his condition all the time. Let it go. We're going on the rocks rapidly now. If mother lives six months more she will survive him. If she dies soon, he might recover but every week makes it less likely. Death I can stand but not this slow torture wherein a good and a strong man tears off little shreds of himself and throws them away.[23]

Olive Steinbeck died in the spring of 1934 and was buried on the day of her death. Steinbeck, following family custom, served as a pall bearer. Following his mother's death, Steinbeck and Carol then continued to care for the older man at his home, while the author struggled on with his writing. In a letter written to a friend, Edith Wagner, Steinbeck relates that he had begun another book:

When we came here over a month ago, I got to work finally and did three-fourths of a book. I thought I was going to slip it through, but dad's decline beat me. This is indeed writing under difficulty. The house in Salinas is pretty haunted now. I see things walking at night that it is not good to see. This last book is a very jolly one about Monterey paisanos. Its tone, I guess, is direct rebellion against all the sorrow of our house. Dad doesn't like characters to swear. But if I had taken all the writing instructions I've been given, I would be insane. I try to write what seems to be true. If it isn't true for other people, then it isn't good art.

But I've only my own eyes to see with. I won't use the eyes of other people. And as long as we can eat and write more books, that's really all I require.[24]

First Success

The work on his new book, *Tortilla Flat*, provided Steinbeck with a welcome creative outlet. "I don't care much whether it amounts to anything," he remarked to Robert Ballou at the time. "I am enjoying it and I need something to help me over this last ditch."[25]

In *Tortilla Flat* Steinbeck attempts to recount a modern version of the Arthurian legend. A Monterey high school teacher named Sue Gregory, who was a close friend of Steinbeck's, greatly encouraged and influenced the book. Gregory and Steinbeck shared a deep affection for the Spanish-speaking people in the central California region. Steinbeck visited her frequently and spent many absorbing hours listening to the cultural anecdotes she had learned over the years.

The "paisanos," as the people of "Tortilla Flat" were often called, lived primarily on the outskirts of town in the hills above Monterey. They were a community whose bloodlines included Italian and Portuguese as well as Spanish and Native American. Steinbeck had for years nourished the idea of composing a book of short stories about the paisanos. He had grown up with them, and his acquaintance with many had led him into their homes and to their supper tables. He had, with Ed Ricketts, spent many evenings cruising the waterfront cafes and bars, enjoying their companionship.

Tortilla Flat renders the stories Steinbeck had heard from Sue Gregory, along with his own experiences, as a current, regional folkloric tale that captures much of the distinctive flavor of the paisano lifestyle. What emerges is a gently humorous and bittersweet story of earthy fellowship.

Tortilla Flat relates the adventures of Danny and his free-spirited vagabond friends. Danny is an army veteran who, in the book's opening, returns home to Monterey to find himself heir to his grandfather's two small houses. Displaying a nobility worthy of King Arthur himself, Danny opens his home to shelter his shiftless but good-hearted companions, and the company embark on a series of adventures that are often hilarious and in the end deeply moving and tragic.

In his short preface to *Tortilla Flat*, Steinbeck made it clear that he wished to draw a distinct parallel between the pathetic adventures of the paisanos in his novel and the deeds of the armored knights errant of the Arthurian saga:

> For Danny's house was not unlike the Round Table, and Danny's friends were not unlike the knights of it. And this is the story of how that group came into being, of how it flourished and grew to be an organization beautiful and wise.[26]

Steinbeck sent the completed manuscript of *Tortilla Flat* to Robert Ballou in the spring of 1934. To Steinbeck's disappointment, Ballou declined to publish it. The writer was told that in Ballou's opinion, *Tortilla Flat* lacked the depth of Steinbeck's earlier books. Steinbeck disagreed. In a letter to Mavis McIntosh, Steinbeck related his thoughts on the Arthurian theme he had wished to convey in *Tortilla Flat:*

A still from the movie version of Tortilla Flat, *a bittersweet tale about a group of free-spirited paisanos.*

I want to write something about *Tortilla Flat* and about some ideas I have about it. The book has a very definite theme. I thought it was clear enough. I have expected that the plan of the Arthurian cycle would be recognized, that my Gawaine and my Launcelot, my Arthur and Galahad would be recognized. Even the incident of the Sangreal in the search of the forest is not clear enough I guess. The form is that of the Malory version [*Morte d'Arthur*], the coming of Arthur and the mystic quality of owning a house, the forming of the round table, the adventure of the knights and finally, the mystic translation of Danny.

However, I seem not to have made any of this clear. The main issue was to present a little known and, to me, delightful people. Is not this cycle story or theme enough? Perhaps it is not enough because I have not made it clear enough. What do you think of putting in an interlocutor, who between each incident interprets the incident, morally, esthetically, historically, but in the same manner of the paisanos themselves?[27]

Steinbeck's literary efforts during this time had not gone entirely unnoticed by other Eastern publishers. Although *Cup of Gold* was by then out of print, the author's two other novels, *The Pastures of Heaven* and *To a God Unknown*, had been read by an enterprising publisher named Pascal Covici, who had come to admire Steinbeck's work.

Covici contacted Steinbeck through McIntosh & Otis, offering to publish *Tor-*

A Humble Resolution

Steinbeck suffered from periods of doubt over his ability as a writer. In 1932 his commitment to maintain the integrity of his writing moved him to write such solemn resolutions as those in this letter to Carlton Sheffield, which appears in Steinbeck: A Life in Letters.

"Now as always—humility and terror. Fear that the working of my pen cannot capture the grinding of my brain. It is so easy to understand why the ancients prayed for the help of a Muse. And the Muse came and stood beside them, and we, heaven help us, do not believe in Muses. We have nothing to fall back on but our craftsmanship and it, as modern literature attests, is inadequate.

May I be honest; may I be decent; may I be unaffected by the technique of hucksters. If invocation is required, let this be my invocation—may I be strong and yet gentle, tender and yet wise, wise and yet tolerant. May I for a little while, only for a little while, see with the inflamed eyes of a God."

In Tortilla Flat *Steinbeck attempted to draw a parallel between the adventures of the paisanos and the knights of the Round Table (pictured).*

tilla Flat and to reprint the author's earlier works. Steinbeck gladly accepted the offer. *Tortilla Flat* had by this time been rejected by five publishers, and Steinbeck was nearly in despair: "I am very much pleased of course," he wrote to Wilbur Needham, book critic for the *Los Angeles Times.* "We have been very close to the end these last couple of years."[28]

Tortilla Flat, published by the printing house of Covici-Friede in New York in 1935, was immediately popular. In the summer of that year, much to Steinbeck's astonishment, the book appeared on the best-seller list and that winter was awarded the prestigious Commonwealth Club of California Gold Medal for the best novel of the year.

Tortilla Flat, Steinbeck's fourth published book in six years, was destined to become his first commercial success and a literary classic.

3 Poverty and Persistence

In 1935, at the age of thirty-three, Steinbeck could look back on a career spanning ten years of struggle during which he had written with professional intent. He had managed to become a published author, but his books had not sold well until the success of *Tortilla Flat*.

Steinbeck was plagued with self-doubt when his first published books failed to sell well. His determination to succeed as a writer helped him overcome these bouts of depression.

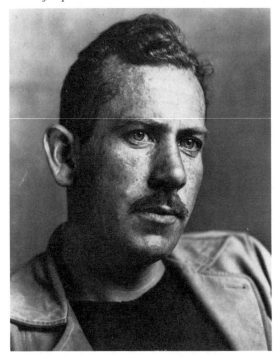

Despite his determination to succeed as a writer, Steinbeck was sometimes discouraged to the point of despair, as indicated in a letter to Amasa Miller in 1931:

> You see the haunting thought comes that perhaps I have been kidding myself and other people—that I have nothing to say or no art in saying nothing. It is two years since I have received the slightest encouragement and that was short-lived.[29]

Despite these periods of depression, Steinbeck was never entirely defeated in his ambition to write. With every hardship that he and Carol endured, Steinbeck's determination to succeed strengthened. Steinbeck persisted in his work and strove to refine his writing into the highest art form he was capable of achieving. During those years of internship Steinbeck's writing matured greatly, as he experimented with numerous writing techniques, themes, and concepts that had helped him to develop a compelling and descriptive narrative style.

Steinbeck strove to write objectively. He conveyed ideas and impressions of characters and situations in an impersonal manner. In this way, Steinbeck hoped to allow readers to perceive and interpret the people and events of his books according

In a letter to Elizabeth Otis, included in The True Adventures of John Steinbeck, Writer, *Steinbeck confides his discomfort with fame and his concern about the possibility of being typecast as a writer.*

"Hotel clerks here are being instructed to tell guests that there is no Tortilla Flat. The Chamber of Commerce does not like my poor efforts I guess. . . . The publicity of TF is rather terrible out here and we may have to run ahead of it. Please ask CF [an unidentified associate of Steinbeck's] not to give my address to anyone. Curious that this second-rate book, written for relaxation, should cause this fuss. People are actually taking it seriously. . . . I'm scared to death of popularity. It has ruined everyone I know. That's one of the reasons I would like *In Dubious Battle* printed next. Myths form quickly and I want no tag of humorist on me, nor any other kind."

---

to their own thoughts and emotions. This objective literary style, along with Steinbeck's vivid descriptive talent, were elements that contributed to the dramatic power of his greatest books.

"A Book Written in Disorder"

Steinbeck's joy in publishing *Tortilla Flat* in 1935 was overshadowed by the death of his father in the same year. On a postcard sent to his godmother Elizabeth Bailey, Steinbeck confided the sorrow he felt over the disappointments his father had suffered:

I should have preferred no service at all for dad. I can think of nothing for him so eloquent as silence. Poor silent man all his life. I feel very badly, not

about his death, but about his life, for he told me only a few months ago that he had never done anything he wanted to do. Worst of all he hadn't done the work he wanted to do.[30]

Steinbeck resolved that he would never abandon the pursuit of his own professional destiny as a writer. The success of *Tortilla Flat* had gained him national renown, but Steinbeck's primary desire was not for fame. He was basically a shy man who disliked being a public figure. Steinbeck preferred privacy and the opportunity to continue his quest to achieve perfection in his writing. He often worked on several books at the same time. Upon completing one, he would simply continue writing the next.

While working on the final revisions of *Tortilla Flat*, Steinbeck had become deeply involved in drafting the manuscript for another novel. This new book was a dramatic departure in style and theme from the regional character studies that represented most of his earlier work. Steinbeck had chosen to title his next novel *In Dubious Battle*. As he said in a letter to his friend George Albee, it was a book "written in disorder."[31]

In Dubious Battle is a stirring chronicle of the bitter labor disputes that inflamed much of rural California during the depression years. Steinbeck had drawn the title of his book from the lines of John Milton's epic poem *Paradise Lost*. Steinbeck believed the poem expressed the love-hate conflict within all of mankind which he felt was particularly dramatized in his own story of the California labor conflicts:

In Dubious Battle *chronicles rural California's bitter labor disputes during the depression years. Here, cotton pickers strike in the San Joaquin Valley, where three died in confrontations between striking agricultural workers and ranch owners.*

Innumerable force of Spirits armed,
That durst dislike his reign, and, me preferring,
In Dubious Battle on the plains of Heaven,
And shook His throne. What though the field be lost?
All is not lost—the unconquerable will,
And Study of revenge, immortal hate,
And courage never to submit or yield:
And what is else not to be overcome?[32]

In Dubious Battle tells the grim and violent story of two Marxist agitators who attempt to organize an agricultural strike in the fictitious Torgas Valley, a strife-ridden farming region supposedly located in central California. Steinbeck had observed the growing antagonism between well-organized farm owners and discontented farm laborers. Steinbeck's sympathies lay with the very low-paid migrant workers, whom he believed were being exploited. He felt no alliance, however, for Communists, who were actively attempting to achieve their political ends by the use of mob violence in labor disputes.

A Battle of Love and Hatred

Steinbeck had spent considerable time during the spring of 1934 in secret correspondence with a Communist agitator who had taken refuge with local sympathizers in the Monterey area. The fugitive's story had fascinated Steinbeck, who painstakingly recorded it with the original intention of writing a journalistic account of the man's subversive activities. Steinbeck soon realized, however, that the story offered greater possibilities as a work of

A Compelling Political Ideology

Many of the convictions regarding labor reform expressed in Steinbeck's novel In Dubious Battle, *including the following excerpt, echoed the beliefs of strike leaders.*

"Plant an idea and let it grow. Let the situation develop and take advantage of opportunities. Don't come on like a great strike leader—stay in the background (the growers are smart and they know enough to get you if you become famous). Talk to people on their own level and let the ideas about what to do come from them. . . . The essence of leadership is not to portray yourself as some sort of know-it-all, but your ability to develop the people you are working with so they themselves can take the initiative and do the organizational drive."

fiction. He believed that if he wrote the book in the terse, objective style of a documentary, he could produce a realistic narrative of electrifying intensity.

Steinbeck's reasons for writing *In Dubious Battle*, then, were philosophical rather than strictly political. In a letter to George Albee, he candidly expressed his creative motive for the book:

> I'm not interested in ranting about justice and oppression, mere outcroppings which indicate the condition. But man hates something in himself. He has been able to defeat every natural obstacle but himself he cannot win over unless he kills every individual. And this self-hate which goes so closely in hand with self-love is what I wrote about.[33]

In Dubious Battle was published in mid-January 1936 and had moderately good sales. Despite its controversial content, the book received favorable reviews from conservative and liberal literary publications alike. This positive response both pleased and surprised Steinbeck, who said in a letter to his agent Elizabeth Otis: "I think the reception IDB [*In Dubious Battle*] seems to be getting is very funny. Instead of being fought by both sides it seems both sides are claiming and protecting it."[34]

In Dubious Battle was a milestone in Steinbeck's literary career. It reveals a maturity of style and discipline. His deft journalistic treatment of the book's grim subject matter produced a social chronicle of forceful vividness.

During negotiations for the publication of *In Dubious Battle*, Steinbeck had corresponded on several occasions with his new publisher Pascal Covici, and a cordial long-distance relationship had developed between the two men. In mid-August of 1935, Steinbeck met Covici in person. Covici, who had come to San Francisco on business, decided to take the opportunity to visit Steinbeck in Pacific Grove and to deliver the author's first royalty check for *Tortilla Flat*. The two men got along well and remained friends throughout Covici's life.

Steinbeck decided to use the funds from his royalty check to finance an extended vacation in Mexico for Carol and himself. The Steinbecks arrived in Mexico City in September 1935 and spent the next three-and-a-half months touring the country. The vacation provided a welcome interlude after the difficult period of financial hardship compounded by the

The movie version of Tortilla Flat, *which starred Spencer Tracy, Hedy Lamarr, and John Garfield, is considered a film classic.*

deaths of Steinbeck's parents: "We just stroll about the streets and get bathed in life," Steinbeck wrote happily in a letter to George Albee. "There has been too much death about us. This well of just pure life is charging us up again."[35]

While still vacationing in Mexico, Steinbeck received a telegram from his agents notifying him that Paramount Studio had purchased the film rights for *Tortilla Flat* for $4,000 and would adapt the novel into a motion picture. The Steinbecks flew to New York in December to sign the film contracts and returned to California to spend Christmas at Pacific Grove. *Tortilla Flat* was released as a film in 1942 and is considered to be a classic by many people today.

A Story of Fate

Encouraged by the success of *Tortilla Flat* and *In Dubious Battle*, Steinbeck began to seriously consider the possibility of having more of his work dramatized for either the theater or motion pictures. Early in 1936, he began work on a new book, which he described in a letter to George Albee as a "tricky little thing designed to teach me to write for the theatre."[36] The story, a simple tale of two itinerant ranch hands, was drafted under the working title of *Something That Happened*.

Steinbeck began the book as an experiment in writing a novel as a play in the hope that a dramatic adaptation of the story would expand the audience for his work. By this time, his books were selling well and his finances had improved considerably. The Steinbecks decided to build a house in a secluded area of the commu-

A Humorous Self-Appraisal

An example of Steinbeck's self-appraisal, included in Steinbeck: A Life in Letters, *is contained in this letter of application written to librarian Ann Hadden, who had sponsored Steinbeck for a literary prize.*

"I have all the vices in a very mild way except that of narcotics, unless coffee and tobacco are classed as narcotics. I have been in jail once for a night a long time ago, a result of a combination of circumstance and a reasonable opinion that I could lick a policeman. The last turned out to be undemonstrable. I don't think the trustees [of the Phelan Award] would be interested but they might. I am married and quarrel violently with my wife and we both enjoy it very much. And last, finished a novel of a hundred and twenty thousand words, three drafts in a little over four months."

nity of Los Gatos, about fifty miles north of Monterey. While Carol supervised the construction of the house, Steinbeck continued to write. Work on his latest book progressed smoothly for several weeks until a mishap occurred one evening that Steinbeck related in a humorous letter to Elizabeth Otis:

> Minor tragedy stalked. My setter pup left alone one night, made confetti of about half of my ms. book. Two months work to do over again. It sets me back. There was no other draft. I was pretty mad but the poor little fellow may have been acting critically. I didn't want to ruin a good dog for a ms. I'm not sure is good at all. He only got an ordinary spanking with his punishment flyswatter. But there's the work to do over from the start.[37]

Steinbeck returned to his desk and began to work again, this time under a new title suggested by Ed Ricketts: *Of Mice and Men.*

Construction on the Steinbecks' house was completed by the end of summer. John and Carol moved into their new home in August 1936, where Steinbeck completed the second draft of *Of Mice and Men.* He sent it off to Pascal Covici in New York, who accepted it immediately and began plans for its publication.

Of Mice and Men relates a brief but unforgettable story about the troubled friendship of two men, George and Lennie, who desperately seek to survive by working as hired hands while dreaming of one day finding their promised land: a small house and farm of their own. The plight of George and Lennie was similar to the dilemma of thousands of unemployed men in America during the Great Depression. The roadways throughout California were filled with impoverished people searching for work as farm hands, fruit pickers, and field workers in the agricultural regions of the state. Steinbeck had often worked in the fields to support himself while he was a college student and had come to know the laborers well. He felt a deep sympathy for their harsh, impoverished existence and admired their stubborn courage and determination to survive.

In *Of Mice and Men* Steinbeck presents two symbolic elements essential to the story. The first symbol is the *highway*. To Steinbeck, the open road symbolized the continuing quest of dispossessed people who hoped to find a new home in which to rebuild their lives. The second symbol was the *river*, which represented the barrier between people and the realization of their dream of a promised land. Steinbeck was an avid student of the Bible and had drawn a parallel example from Old Testament references to the River Jordan, which separated the Hebrews from the land of Canaan.

The Valor of Dreams

Of Mice and Men begins on the symbolic highway. The story takes readers from the highway down to "a path through the willows," to their first encounter with George and Lennie, who have followed the path to drink from the green waters of a deep pool, concealed by the trees below. *Of Mice and Men* tells of their quest to find sanctuary from poverty, cruelty, and hardship. Ever hopeful, Lennie envisions the day "when we get that little place an' live on the fatta the lan'."[38]

Lennie, a big, good-hearted man who is mentally retarded, is unable to control his enormous physical strength and childlike impulses. Because of his mental hand-

Dust bowl farm refugees set out toward California in search of work. Such men inspired Steinbeck in his creation of the characters George and Lennie in Of Mice and Men.

In the movie version of Of Mice and Men, *actor Lon Chaney Jr. (standing) starred as the big-hearted, but mentally retarded Lennie, and Burgess Meredith (left corner) played George, Lennie's friend and guardian.*

icap, Lennie has, according to George, done some "bad things." Townspeople who had been frightened by Lennie's bizarre behavior had driven the two men away from their last job. During their travels Lennie has acquired a mouse, which he cherishes as a pet. The animal symbolizes the fragile dream the two friends share of a happy future.

George is a small but intelligent man who acts as Lennie's guardian. When Lennie accidentally crushes the mouse in his hand, George, irritated by his friend's clumsiness, throws the animal away in a gesture that suggests the eventual loss of their own dream. The two men find employment at a nearby ranch. For a brief time, they enjoy the hope of one day having their own home, but the dream is never realized because of the failings of both men. Ultimately George acknowledges his own incurable vagrancy:

I'll work my month an' I'll take my fifty bucks an' I'll stay all night in some lousy cat house. An' then I'll come back an' work another month an' I'll have fifty bucks more.[39]

At the end, Lennie, in bewildered panic, kills a woman in much the same way he had crushed the mouse. Fleeing from a posse, the two friends once again take refuge at the green pool, where George sorrowfully draws a pistol: "Look acrost the river, Lennie, an' I'll tell you so you can almost see it" [the farm they had dreamed of].[40] Unaware of what is about to happen, Lennie happily obeys, still dreaming of a new life when the gun is fired.

In *Of Mice and Men* Steinbeck stresses the philosophical principle of "nonteleology," which was to characterize much of his writing. This theory counters the doctrine of teleology, or the belief in

A Writer's Inner Wealth

Steinbeck believed that the greatest reward derived from writing was the joy of writing itself. In a letter written to Henry Jackson in 1935, found in Steinbeck: A Life in Letters, *the author explained the creative motivation for his work that was to remain with him throughout his life.*

"In the last few books I have felt a curious richness as though my life had been multiplied through having become identified in a most real way with people who are not me. I have loved that. And I am afraid, terribly afraid, that if the bars ever go down, if I become a trade mark, I shall lose the ability to do that. When I do stop I shall stop working because it won't be fun any more. The work has been the means of making me feel that I am living richly, diversely, and, in a few cases and for a few moments, even heroically. All of these things are not me, for I am none of these things. But sometimes in my own mind at least I can create something which is larger and richer than I am. In this aspect I suppose my satisfaction is much like that of a father who sees his son succeed where he has failed. Not being brave I am glad when I can make a brave person whom I believe in."

providence and the ability of people to determine their future, asserting instead the fatalistic belief that the world is vast and indifferent, and people must adapt in the best way they can. The heroism of this struggle to adapt and to survive was often the basis of Steinbeck's stories. The valor to dream of what was apparently unachievable was an aspect of human character that to Steinbeck was noble and enduring.

Of Mice and Men was published in 1937. The book became an immediate best-seller and is one of Steinbeck's most popular and widely read novels. In the spring of 1937, Steinbeck collaborated with playwright-director George S. Kaufman to write the script for a theater adaptation of *Of Mice and Men*. The play was produced on Broadway in 1937 and received the New York Drama Critics' Circle Award, given by a distinguished association of drama critics for the best American play of the season.

Years later, when plans were being made to produce *Of Mice and Men* as a musical, Steinbeck expressed these thoughts in a letter to his friend Annie Laurie Williams, who was also a theatrical agent with McIntosh & Otis:

"M&M" may seem to be unrelieved tragedy, but it is not. . . . Everyone in the world has a dream he knows can't come off but he spends his life hoping it may. This is at once sadness, and the greatness and the triumph of our species.[41]

4 An Exalted Endeavor

While completing the final draft for *Of Mice and Men* in August 1936, Steinbeck was visited at his home by an old friend named George West, chief editorial writer for the *San Francisco News*. West offered Steinbeck an assignment to research and write a series of newspaper articles on migrant farm labor in California. The task involved traveling to the agricultural regions of central California, particularly the San Joaquin Valley, to report on the living conditions of the migrant workers and the state of the rural boarding facilities called sanitary camps, which were provided for

the workers by the federal government. Steinbeck was asked to write firsthand observations of the farmers known as "Okies," who had left their drought-stricken farms in the Dust Bowl of Oklahoma to seek new homes in California.

Steinbeck, who was free of commitment to any other particular work, decided to accept the assignment. He began researching the story in late summer of 1936 by visiting the migrant camp of Weedpatch, built at Arvin, near Bakersfield, California. To study the migrant workers as inconspicuously as possible,

While researching his assignment for the San Francisco News, *Steinbeck visited government-run migratory camps to study the living and working conditions of the migrant workers.*

A Reluctant Celebrity

When Of Mice and Men *was produced as a play in 1938, Steinbeck was uncomfortable making public appearances. A letter to Elizabeth Otis written in May 1938 and included in* Steinbeck: A Life in Letters *reveals the author's self-consciousness.*

"I guess I just haven't any social sense. So many things can happen. I have never submitted a novel to the Commonwealth Club [a literary organization] here which gives a medal every year but Pat [Covici] has [usually made a submission for me]. This year he forgot to or something and I understand that it is being spread that I think I am too good to compete in local things now. Just little things like that all the time. And this not going to New York to see this play [Of Mice and Men] which is being used everywhere now (it has got to the fourth-rate movie columnists by now). I'd like to see the play but I wouldn't go six thousand miles to see the opening of the second coming of Christ. Why is it so damned important?"

Steinbeck dressed in worn clothing and drove an old bakery truck outfitted in a manner similar to many of the vehicles in which the laborers traveled.

During his visit to Weedpatch, Steinbeck met Tom Collins, a federal employee who had been assigned to organize the Arvin sanitary camp. Steinbeck spent several days with Collins observing the camp operations and attending camp committee meetings and one of the weekend dances. In addition, Steinbeck accompanied Collins on an inspection tour of several squatters' camps outside Arvin, where many migrant workers lived.

Steinbeck witnessed the severe hardships the migrant families endured as they labored long hours in the fields and received wages that barely enabled them to feed their families. He saw how many local farm owners, armed with rifles and ax handles, tried to frighten and scatter the workers to prevent them from effectively organizing labor strikes. Steinbeck was deeply impressed by Collins, who proved to be an energetic organizer committed to improving the plight of the laborers. Above all, however, Steinbeck was moved by the heroism of the migrants themselves, as they faced violence, starvation, and wretched living conditions.

Before leaving Arvin, Collins gave Steinbeck several detailed reports of his experiences as a camp manager. Included were stories Collins had recorded from his observations of camp life as well as the words to several songs sung by the migrants. Then, having completed his research visit to the sanitary camps, Steinbeck returned to Pacific Grove to write his articles.

The material from Collins proved invaluable to Steinbeck in composing articles that accurately and vividly captured the feeling and spirit of the migrant workers' life. Shortly after his return from Arvin, Steinbeck wrote to Collins, expressing his appreciation for the federal agent's generous aid:

I want to thank you for one of the very fine experiences of a life. But I think you know exactly how I feel about it. I hope I can be of some kind of help. On the other hand I don't want to be presumptuous. In the articles I shall be very careful to try to do some good and no harm.[42]

Prelude to a Novel

Steinbeck's work was published in the *San Francisco News* in October 1936 as a week-long series of articles under the title "The Harvest Gypsies." The articles eloquently expressed Steinbeck's admiration for the migrant workers and powerfully described the adversity they suffered.

After completing his assignment for the *San Francisco News*, Steinbeck continued his research and began to consider other possible means of publishing material on the migrants' plight. At the migrant camps that summer, Steinbeck developed a deep sense of anger over the injustices he had witnessed.

The winter of 1937 brought heavy rains and flooding to the agricultural region of Visalia, California, where thousands of farm workers had migrated in search of jobs. Steinbeck received a request from the federal Farm Security Administration to go to Visalia and report his observations. Steinbeck contacted Tom Collins once again and the two men traveled to the stricken area, where they spent ten days together offering relief assistance to the migrants. During this time *Life* magazine assigned a staff photographer to record the conditions in Visalia for a proposed article to be written by Steinbeck.

In a letter to his agent Elizabeth Otis written shortly after his return from the

A squatter family in Visalia receives immunization shots. At the request of the Farm Security Administration, Steinbeck agreed to visit Visalia and report his observations.

flooded regions, Steinbeck expressed his emotional involvement with the beleaguered migrants:

> Just got back from another week in the field. The floods have aggravated the starvation and sickness. I went down for *Life* this time. *Fortune* [magazine] wanted me to do an article for them but I won't. I don't like the audience. Then *Life* sent me down with a photographer from its staff and we took a lot of pictures of the people.
>
> It is the most heartbreaking thing in the world. If *Life* does use the stuff there will be lots of pictures and swell ones. It will give you an idea of the kind of people they are and the kind of faces, I break myself [give away all the money I'm carrying] every time I go out because the argument that one person's effort can't really do anything doesn't seem to apply when you come on a bunch of starving children and you have a little money.[43]

The article was submitted to *Life* magazine, but the editors felt that much of the language was inflammatory. Steinbeck, concerned that the story would lose its impact, refused to tone down his words, and the article was rejected. Steinbeck was determined to publish the article as he had written it, and in April 1938 he arranged to have it published in another California newspaper, the *Monterey Trader*. The story

Steinbeck witnessed firsthand the sad plight of the migrant families, who toiled long hours in the fields for meager wages, and were forced to endure wretched living conditions.

appeared under the title "Starvation Under the Orange Trees" and despite the *Trader's* relatively modest circulation, generated great sympathy for the flood victims.

The Purging of Anger

Steinbeck's involvement with the California migrant workers inspired him to choose the subject of his next novel. Since the publication of *Of Mice and Men*, Steinbeck had been excited by the idea of writing what he described to friends as the "big book." He had looked forward to achieving the financial security that would enable him to undertake the writing of a book that would be a crowning artistic accomplishment in his literary career.

Encouraged by the success of *Tortilla Flat*, *In Dubious Battle*, and *Of Mice and Men*, Steinbeck felt that he now had the opportunity to direct his energies toward this ambitious literary undertaking. Steinbeck was intensely angered by the unjust treatment of the migrants he had seen in the San Joaquin Valley and in his own hometown of Salinas. He decided to make the plight of the migrant workers the theme of this major book.

Steinbeck began work on a novel entitled *L'Affaire Lettuceberg*, in which he attacked acts of clandestine violence sanctioned or committed by some of the prominent Salinas growers. "It is a mean, nasty book, and if I could make it nastier I would," wrote Steinbeck to Elizabeth Otis in May 1938.[44] After several weeks of work on the manuscript, Steinbeck had relieved much of his anger and had developed a different perspective on his work, which he shared in another letter to Elizabeth Otis:

Not once in the writing of it *[L'Affaire Lettuceberg]* have I felt the curious warm pleasure that comes when work is going well. My whole work drive has been aimed at making people understand each other and then I deliberately write this book, the aim of which is to cause hatred through partial understanding. My father would have called it a smart-alec book. It was full of tricks to make people ridiculous. If I can't do better I have slipped badly.[45]

Shortly afterward, Steinbeck destroyed the manuscript for *L'Affaire Lettuceberg* and began a new novel on the migrant laborers focusing primarily on the Okies and their desperate pilgrimage to find work in the California farmlands. He decided to focus on his admiration of the Okies' heroism rather than his hatred of exploitive farm owners. Steinbeck began his new novel inspired with a renewed sense of positive direction and creative confidence. In June 1938 he wrote to Elizabeth Otis, expressing his enthusiasm:

This is a very happy time. The new book is going well. Too fast. I'm having to hold it down. I don't want it to go so fast for fear the tempo will be fast and this is a plodding, crawling book. So I'm holding it down to approximately six pages a day . . . .

Anyway it is a nice thing to be working and believing in my work again. I hope I can keep the drive all fall. I like it. I only feel whole and well when it is this way. I don't yet understand what happened or why the bad book should have cleared the air so completely for this one. I am simply glad that it is so.[46]

While working on his new book, Steinbeck learned that Pascal Covici, his editor and publisher, had been forced to declare bankruptcy for his publishing company, Covici-Friede. As soon as this news was released, Steinbeck was approached by several publishers with offers to buy his next book. Steinbeck loyally refused all proposals. He instead assisted Covici in securing a position as an editor at Viking Press, with the understanding that Steinbeck would continue working with Covici under contract to Viking. In gratitude, Covici sent Steinbeck a telegram:

> I shall never be able to repay you for this magnificent support you gave me and now you are with me at the Viking where with no other financial worries to harass and embarrass me I shall continue as your honored and happy publisher.[47]

At his wife's suggestion, Steinbeck decided to call the new novel *The Grapes of Wrath*. Carol worked with Steinbeck for many exhausting months, typing and editing the manuscript as her husband feverishly continued to write new chapters. The novel was completed in the fall of 1938 and Steinbeck mailed it off to McIntosh & Otis, along with a letter that reflected the writer's great excitement:

> This afternoon by express we are sending you the manuscript of *The Grapes of Wrath*. We hope to God you like it. Will you let us know first that you received it and second what you think of it.[48]

Steinbeck was extremely proud of this book although he was sure that it would never be popular. He believed that the novel's grim content would not appeal to a large audience. This skepticism was expressed in a letter written in November 1938 in which Steinbeck requested that Elizabeth Otis help persuade Pascal ("Pat") Covici, at Viking, to print only a small edition of *The Grapes of Wrath*:

The Matter of an Author's Privacy

Elated by the success of The Grapes of Wrath, *Pat Covici asked Steinbeck in February 1939 for the book's original manuscript. In this letter included in* Steinbeck: A Life in Letters, *Steinbeck replied to his editor's request.*

"I keep having to say no all the time and I hate it. It's about the manuscript this time. You see I feel that this is Carol's so I gave her [his wife] the manuscript. For myself I don't like anything personal to intrude on this or any other book but this one in particular. I think a book should be itself, complete and in print. What went into the writing of it is no business of the reader. I disapprove of having my crabbed hand exposed. The fact that my writing is small may be a marvel, but it is also completely unimportant to the book. No, I want this book to be itself with no history and no writer."

The movie version of The Grapes of Wrath *starred Henry Fonda as Tom Joad, the main character in Steinbeck's stirring chronicle of the dispossessed Dust Bowl farmers of Oklahoma.*

Look Elizabeth I want to make something very clear and I want you to help with it. Pat talked in terms of very large first editions of this next book *[The Grapes of Wrath]*. I want to go on record as advising against it. This will not be a popular book.[49]

After reading the manuscript, however, Covici believed that Steinbeck had written a great American epic. He was convinced that *The Grapes of Wrath* would be a huge success and proceeded to publish a large first edition. Steinbeck by this time had earned a notable literary reputation from the popular success of *Tortilla Flat, In Dubious Battle,* and *Of Mice and Men.* Yet the tremendous public response to *The Grapes of Wrath* soon surpassed the popularity of those earlier books. By the time *The Grapes of Wrath* was published in April, advance sales had reached a total of ninety thousand copies. Covici's faith in the book was justified.

An American Epic

The Grapes of Wrath is a stirring chronicle of the dispossessed Dust Bowl farmers of Oklahoma. Steinbeck opens his saga with a description of southern farm country reduced by drought to a wasteland. Along the barren highway, a solitary man, Tom Joad, is returning home to his family, having served a prison sentence for killing a man in a personal dispute. He is joined by Jim Casy, a disillusioned preacher who has abandoned his ministry: "The sperit," he tells Joad, "ain't in the people much no more; and worse'n that, the sperit ain't in me no more."[50]

The two men travel together to the Joad farm to find the family gone, the property abandoned, the house a deserted shambles. There remains only a lean, gray cat who prowls the ruins. From a destitute neighbor named Muley Graves, Tom and Casey learn that the Joads, like hundreds of

The film featured actress Jane Darwell (bottom left) as Ma Joad, who struggles to keep the family together during the long, difficult journey.

their neighbors, have been "tractored off" and driven from their land by a bureaucratic monster of organized finance known only as "the Bank."

The farmers, however, sense that a greater and more threatening power is driving them away. The Bank, they feel, has sinister allies, but the people cannot fight what they do not know, so they must go. When Tom is reunited with his family, who have gathered at his Uncle John's property, he finds that papers have also been served on his uncle's farm. The entire family is preparing to journey to California in search of work. A handbill acquired by Pa Joad advertises a need for harvesters and offers the family hope for a new beginning.

Although he will be violating the conditions of his parole, Tom decides to join the family on the journey west. Reverend Casey also accompanies the Joads. Tom's father, who has been devastated by the loss of the land, feels that he has lost something of his manhood as well. Thus it falls to Ma Joad to assume the role of active head of the family: "All we got is the family unbroken," she declares.[51] The events of their long, hard journey serve as markers on a path of realization. Through the eventual death and defection of certain members of her family and the suffering and heroism she witnesses in the lives of other migrants encountered on the road, Ma Joad attains a higher understanding of the meaning of family as a unit of mankind: "Use' ta be the family was fust. It ain't so now. It's anybody. Worse off we get, the more we got to do."[52]

The family reaches California only to find themselves part of a vast pilgrimage of other laborers desperately seeking work in the farmlands. As they travel from one migrant camp to another, the Joads discover that the handbill was part of a ruse by farm owners to draw multitudes of workers to California, where they could be exploited as cheap labor.

In addition to grueling hours of low-paying harvest work, the migrants are at times threatened by thugs hired by the big farm owners to suppress any organized attempt by the laborers to improve their conditions. In this relentless struggle for survival, Reverend Jim Casy and Tom Joad are ultimately drawn to factions among the migrants determined to form a labor union.

During a violent confrontation between migrant workers and organized farm owners aided by hired henchmen, Jim Casy is killed and Tom is forced to flee for his life after killing a man in self-defense. The heroic sacrifice of Casy and the injustice Tom has witnessed impel Tom to keep alive the struggle against economic oppression.

Tom realizes that he is now a fugitive from the law and must leave his family. He bids farewell to his mother, who has come to his hiding place to bring him food. In spite of the sorrow they share over his de-

A Stand for Creative Integrity

Steinbeck's editors asked for a rewrite of the closing scene in The Grapes of Wrath, *in which Rose of Sharon offers her breast milk to a starving man. Included in* The True Adventures of John Steinbeck, Writer *is a letter to Pat Covici, in which Steinbeck refuses to change the ending.*

"I have your letter today. And I am sorry but I cannot change that ending. It is casual—there is no fruity climax, it is not more important than any other part of the book—if there is a symbol, it is a survival symbol not a love symbol, it must be an accident, it must be a stranger, and it must be quick.

. . . The giving of the breast has no more sentiment than the giving of a piece of bread . . . I know that books lead to a strong deep climax. This one doesn't except by implication and the reader must bring the implication to it. If he doesn't, it wasn't a book for him to read. Throughout I've tried to make the reader participate in the actuality, what he takes from it will be scaled entirely on his own depth or hollowness. There are five layers in this book; a reader will find as many as he can and he won't find more than he has in himself."

parture, Tom reassures his mother that he will always be with the people in spirit:

> Then I'll be aroun' in the dark. I'll be ever'where—wherever you look. Wherever they's a fight so hungry people can eat, I'll be there. Wherever they's a cop beat'n up a guy, I'll be there. If Casy knowed, why, I'll be in the way guys yell when they're mad an'—I'll be in the way kids laugh when they're hungry an' they know supper's ready. An' when our folks eat the stuff they raise an' live in the houses they build—why I'll be there. See? God, I'm talkin' like Casy. Comes of thinkin' about him so much. Seems like I can see him sometimes.[53]

A Controversial Classic

The Grapes of Wrath was published in 1939 and in the spring became the number one best-seller in the country. Along with its great popular success, however, the book generated national controversy over the horrifying living conditions of the migrants. Critics condemned portions of the book for its strong language. Charges of filth were leveled against the novel, which was banned in several regions of the country, including Buffalo, New York, East Saint Louis, Illinois, and Kern County, California. The most serious attacks on the novel, however, were from numerous political factions of organized farm owners who accused Steinbeck of distorting the truth about the treatment of farm laborers, while others denounced the book as communist propaganda.

The book, however, was also championed by such prominent figures as author Pearl Buck, who publicly praised it, and Eleanor Roosevelt, wife of President Franklin D. Roosevelt, who toured the migrant camps and corroborated the book's accuracy in several statements to the press. In gratitude for her support, Steinbeck wrote to Mrs. Roosevelt:

> May I thank you for your words. I have been called a liar so constantly that sometimes I wonder whether I may not have dreamed the things I saw and heard in the period of my research.[54]

Despite the great controversy caused by *The Grapes of Wrath*, government reform programs to improve the working and living conditions of farm laborers would not be effected for many years. Publication of Steinbeck's novel had raised public consciousness regarding the plight of the migrants and prompted hearings by the Senate Committee on Education and Labor to investigate violations of laborers' civil rights. America's entry into World War II in 1941, however, obscured the issue as the government tried to rally the support of organized farm growers to raise food for the national war effort.

Although Steinbeck was proud of *The Grapes of Wrath*, he was uncomfortable with the novel's tremendous commercial success and the fame it brought him. Steinbeck was an intensely private man who had no desire to be a celebrity. A reflective journal entry Steinbeck wrote nearly a year after the publication of *Grapes of Wrath* reveals in some degree the great stress he experienced upon becoming known as the author of a best-selling book:

> It is one year ago less ten days that I finished the first draft of the *Grapes*. . . . This is a year without writing (except for little jobs—mechanical fixings).

A Cry of Outrage

In The Grapes of Wrath *Steinbeck wrote with angry eloquence about a rage he believed to be shared by thousands of migrant workers over their common plight.*

"There is a crime here that goes beyond denunciation. There is a sorrow here that weeping cannot symbolize. There is a failure here that topples all our success. The fertile earth, the straight tree rows, the sturdy trunks, and the ripe fruit. And children dying of pellagra must die because a profit cannot be taken from an orange. And coroners must fill in the certificates—died of malnutrition—because the food must rot, must be forced to rot.

The people come with nets to fish for potatoes in the river, and the guards hold them back; they come in rattling cars to get the dumped oranges, but the kerosene is sprayed. And they stand still and watch the potatoes float by, listen to the screaming pigs being killed in a ditch and covered with quicklime, watch the mountains of oranges slop down to a putrefying ooze; and in the eyes of the people there is failure; and in the eyes of the hungry there is a growing wrath. In the souls of the people the grapes of wrath are filling and growing heavy, growing heavy for the vintage."

In this 1937 photo, photographer Dorothea Lange captured the desperation of a young Oklahoma mother stranded penniless in California.

Due to its controversial subject matter, The Grapes of Wrath *received both praise and criticism. One supporter was First Lady Eleanor Roosevelt, who toured the migrant camps and corroborated the book's accuracy.*

The longest time I've been in many years without writing. The time has come for orientation. What has happened and what it has done to me. In the first place the *Grapes* got really out of hand, became a public hysteria and I became a public domain. I've fought that consistently but I don't know how successfully.[55]

Steinbeck was relieved when *Grapes of Wrath* slipped to number two on the best-seller list in the autumn of 1939. "One nice thing to think of is the speed of obscurity," he wrote to Elizabeth Otis in October 1939. "*Grapes* is not first now. In a month it will be off the list and in six months I'll be forgotten."[56]

The Dust Bowl years were coming to an end. When Steinbeck told his agent that he welcomed the loss of his celebrity status, he had no idea that *The Grapes of Wrath* would inspire generations of readers as a powerful social commentary and a great classic in American literature.

5 Eventful Years

Publication of *Grapes of Wrath* brought Steinbeck national fame as an author. By the time the novel appeared in print in 1939, Steinbeck had written nine books including three best-sellers. As the decade of the 1930s drew to a close, Steinbeck focused his attention to new directions in his writing.

The immense task of writing *Grapes of Wrath* had left Steinbeck physically and emotionally exhausted. Three years of intense work on the creation of the book had taken an extreme toll. In this weakened condition, Steinbeck fell ill with an infected leg. On New Year's Day, 1939, he wrote his editor Pat Covici a letter from his sickbed:

> I'm laid low for the first time in twenty years. Have to stay in bed for two weeks. I think I worked myself past the danger point on that book *[The Grapes of Wrath]*. Broke out in a neuritis and only a basal metabolism test showed the reason.[57]

While Steinbeck convalesced at home in Los Gatos, he began to discuss with Ed Ricketts plans to embark on a cruise along the coastal waters of Baja California to collect and study sea life specimens. Steinbeck and Ricketts planned to compose a handbook of marine biology from the material gathered in their research.

By March 1939, Steinbeck and Ricketts had acquired the necessary travel and research permits from the Mexican government for their venture. They departed for Mexico to engage a boat, enlist a research crew, and outfit the expedition. Steinbeck decided to contract the *Western Flyer* for

After spending many hours with Ed Ricketts (pictured) in his laboratory, Steinbeck developed an interest in marine biology.

"No Punches Were Pulled"

Steinbeck was pleased with the film versions of The Grapes of Wrath *and* Of Mice and Men. *Included in* Steinbeck: A Life in Letters *are his impressions of the two films, which he shared in a letter to Elizabeth Otis.*

"Pictures—We went down in the afternoon and that evening saw *Grapes* at Twentieth-Century [Fox]. [Studio head and producer Darryl F.] Zanuck has more than kept his word. He has a hard, straight picture in which the actors are submerged so completely that it looks and feels like a documentary film and certainly it has a hard, truthful ring. No punches were pulled—in fact, with descriptive matter removed, it is a harsher thing than the book, by far. It seems unbelievable but it is true. The next afternoon we went to see *Mice* and it is a beautiful job. . . . It hangs together and is underplayed. You will like it."

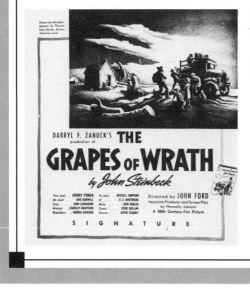

(Left) An advertisement for the 20th Century Fox production of The Grapes of Wrath. *(Below) A movie still from* Of Mice and Men, *which starred Burgess Meredith, Betty Field, and Lon Chaney Jr. (left to right).*

the voyage, and to hire her owner, Tony Berry. The *Western Flyer* was a clean and well-maintained craft, and Steinbeck was impressed by its 165-horsepower, six-cylinder Atlas diesel engine.

On March 11, 1939, the *Western Flyer* departed Monterey Bay for the Gulf of Mexico with Steinbeck, his wife Carol, and Ed Ricketts aboard. The rest of the party consisted of the boat's captain, Tony Berry, and three crew members. Steinbeck was intensely excited about the expedition. He felt that the voyage would give him an opportunity to explore a new avenue for his writing.

With Ed Ricketts's encouragement, Steinbeck had developed a keen interest in scientific research, particularly in the field of marine biology. The two friends had spent many hours in Ricketts's laboratory in Monterey, discussing the scientific philosophy of ecology and its assertion of the interrelation of all living creatures in nature. Steinbeck welcomed the challenge of studying marine ecology along the coast of Baja California and was eager to record his observations in book form.

Steinbeck's party traveled the Mexican gulf waters for six weeks, collecting thousands of specimens and conscientiously logging their discoveries in a journal of notes to be incorporated in the handbook. The expedition ended on April 20, 1940, when the *Western Flyer* returned to Monterey. Steinbeck then began the task of completing the text for the book in collaboration with Ed Ricketts.

The events of the expedition, along with the scientific conclusions of Steinbeck and Ricketts regarding their research, were published by Viking Press in 1941 under the title *The Log from "The Sea of Cortez."* Be-

cause of the scholarly content of the book, *The Sea of Cortez* generated only mild public interest and moderate sales at the time of its release. Steinbeck, however, was proud of the book and the scientific research it chronicled. An excerpt from a letter written in 1963 to a literary correspondent named William Gilgry reveals Steinbeck's fondness for this book:

> I am glad you like the Sea of Cortez. It was little noticed when it appeared but it seems to grow on people. Such a book can't be sold. It has to creep by itself.[58]

During the period of working on *The Sea of Cortez*, Steinbeck had developed an interest in filmmaking. He decided to form a company in association with his editor, Pascal Covici, and his publisher, Harold Guinzburg, for the purpose of producing a semidocumentary motion picture based on *The Forgotten Village*, a short book Steinbeck had written. The plot focuses on the con-

A still from the semi-documentary film based on Steinbeck's The Forgotten Village, *a short story set in a small Mexican village.*

flict of moral values in a small Mexican village when the traditional superstitions of its culture are challenged by scientific and modern medical technology.

While Carol remained in New York, Steinbeck departed for Mexico in October 1940, to serve as a production consultant on the film. Steinbeck was determined that the film present an accurate depiction of life in a Mexican village: "We're getting a picture on film—one of the first times a Mexican pueblito [little town] has been photographed," he wrote to Max Wagner. "I hope it is good. I know it is true—so true that in direction we don't say 'Do this!' but 'Do as you always do.' And what natural actors they [the Mexican villagers] are."[59]

The Forgotten Village was published as a book and released as a motion picture in 1941. Although the film received favorable reviews, national excitement over the entry of the United States into World War II hindered the motion picture's distribution and limited book sales.

Fame and the Pulitzer Prize

In the spring of 1940 Steinbeck received by telephone the news that he had won the Pulitzer Prize in fiction for *The Grapes of Wrath*. Steinbeck learned that Carl Sandburg had been awarded the Pulitzer Prize for history and that William Saroyan had won the drama prize for *The Time of Your Life* but had declined the award. Steinbeck wrote a letter to Joseph Henry Jackson, who had initiated the phone call, expressing his reaction to the news:

Bill [William Saroyan] knows what he wants to do and I don't see that it is anybody's business. His motives and his impulses are his own private property. Do you want a quote from me? I suppose I must say something. If you want to print it, fine. Might go something like this.

"While in the past, I have sometimes been dubious about Pulitzer choices I am pleased and flattered to be chosen in a year when Sandburg and Saroyan were chosen. It is good company." That's the end of the quote. And it is one of the few times when tact and truth seem to be side by side.[60]

Steinbeck had closely followed the news coverage of events in Europe in the opening months of World War II. In early October 1941, Steinbeck responded to a letter from the U.S. Foreign Information Service (FIS) requesting that he attend a conference in Washington, D.C. The FIS had been organized to recruit notable American journalists, novelists, playwrights, and other people in the communications industries such as film and radio, with a view to obtaining their suggestions on how to develop effective anti-Nazi propaganda. When Steinbeck arrived for the conference he found such noted writers as Thornton Wilder and Stephen Vincent Benét also in attendance.

Steinbeck accepted an assignment by the FIS to write an episodic tale titled *The Moon Is Down*, dramatizing the underground activities of patriots in a small European town occupied by Nazis. Written originally as a screenplay, *The Moon Is Down* was published as a novel in 1942 and was Steinbeck's first attempt to chronicle the war. Although not written as overt anti-Nazi propaganda, *The Moon Is Down* became very popular among resistance

An Unrelenting Tale of War

Steinbeck's fascination with the activities of underground resistance groups during World War II led to his willingness to write the novel The Moon Is Down. *Steinbeck's gift for vivid description conveyed a taut and grim chronicle of events of a small European village occupied by enemy troops.*

"Thus it came about that the conquerors grew afraid of the conquered and their nerves wore thin and they shot at shadows in the night. The cold, sullen silence was with them always. Then three soldiers went insane in a week and cried all night and all day until they were sent away home. And others might have gone insane if they had not heard that mercy deaths await the insane at home, and a mercy death is a terrible thing to think of. Fear crept in on the men in their billets and it made them sad, and it crept into the patrols and it made them cruel.

The year turned and the nights grew long. It was dark at three o'clock in the afternoon and not light again until nine in the morning. The jolly lights did not shine on the snow, for by law every window must be black against the bombers. And yet when the English bombers came over, some light always appeared near the coal mine. Sometimes the sentries shot a man with a lantern and once a girl with a flashlight. And it did no good. Nothing was cured by the shooting."

movements throughout Nazi-occupied Europe. In mid-May 1942, Steinbeck was offered another government assignment, which the writer described in a letter to Webster Street:

> I'm going to write a book for the Air Corps on bombers and bomber crews. Beginning Monday I am going from one training camp to another and I'm going to live with the kids and find out what the air corps is about and then do a book with pictures in it.[61]

The resulting book was a factual volume titled *Bombs Away*, which describes in documentary form the rigorous training of a bomber crew. The narrative concludes with the unit's takeoff on its first combat mission. In addition, Steinbeck agreed to write several radio broadcasts for the FIS. His marriage to Carol in the meantime had deteriorated and the two decided to separate. They had often quarreled bitterly over what Carol felt was Steinbeck's neglect as he grew increasingly absorbed in his writing as a means of escaping the stress of fame. Steinbeck was greatly troubled over the turmoil that had overtaken his life. He expressed his unhappiness in a brief entry of a journal he had begun when writing *The Grapes of Wrath:*

Emotionally I am pretty much messed up too. The old trouble of restlessness . . . Carol feeling lone and lost. . . . My own change of temperament seems pretty radical.[62]

Relations grew even more strained when Steinbeck began to be seen frequently in the company of a young singer named Gwyndolyn Conger. Steinbeck had been introduced to Gwyndolyn at a social gathering by his friend Max Wagner in 1940, and a deep friendship had developed between them.

Carol's jealousy over Steinbeck's relationship with Gwyndolyn intensified the anger she felt toward her husband, and she filed for divorce in March 1942. Steinbeck

A wedding picture of John and Gwendolyn taken in New Orleans, where the couple was married in 1943.

reluctantly agreed but felt great regret over the decision. He confided his feelings in a letter to Webster Street in February 1942:

> I don't want to chisel in any way from Carol. I want to give her everything I can. I don't think she will be single long. She will have a lump of money and she is very pretty. I hope to goodness she is happy. Ed [Ricketts] writes that she seems to be having a good time with the Army set. I hope so. The complaint is just. I was cruel to her physically and mentally and she was cruel to me the same way and neither of us could help it.
>
> I am sad at the passage of a good big slice of my life. It could have been ecstatic. That was the age for it. But I still have energy and I am still capable of loving a woman very much. So it isn't really too late for either of us.
>
> It's the first divorce our family ever had and it makes me sad.[63]

Under California law, one year had to elapse before a final divorce decree was issued. During this time, Steinbeck's affection for Gwyndolyn Conger had deepened, and the couple resolved to be married as soon as his divorce was finalized.

Service as a War Correspondent

The unhappiness of his personal life and concern over the unfolding events of World War II had made Steinbeck increasingly restless. His most characteristic method of handling personal conflicts was to seek refuge in his work and to focus on his writing. Steinbeck had done this, for

"I Make Messes Everywhere"

Steinbeck's bitter estrangement from his wife Carol had placed a great strain on his life. Included in Steinbeck: A Life in Letters *is a simultaneously objective and self-pitying letter written to Pascal Covici, in which Steinbeck revealed some of the mental depression he was suffering during this period.*

"My personal life is a curious thing which I won't permit myself to think about yet. I don't want it to get important until I have finished this work. And don't worry about my cracking up. I won't. You'll get the book [The Log from "The Sea of Cortez"] and you won't be ashamed of it, I don't think, although you will probably be pretty much scorned and excoriated for having printed it. Because it does attack some very sacred things, but not at all viciously. Rather with good humor which may be much more devastating.

You say that you hope all will be well with me. That is a nice thing to hope although you know it won't and can't be. I haven't a hell of a lot more time but I have some. I make messes everywhere but I guess everyone does only with some people they don't show. So don't worry about me. I can see myself pretty objectively and the picture is a little silly."

example, when he wrote *Tortilla Flat* during the last months of his parents' lives. While waiting for the completion of his divorce proceedings, Steinbeck applied for a job as a war correspondent with the New York *Herald Tribune*.

In March 1943, the final divorce decree was issued. Steinbeck and Gwyndolyn were married eleven days later in New Orleans. The following month, Steinbeck was notified that the War Department had accredited him as war correspondent with the *Herald Tribune*.

In June 1943, Steinbeck departed for England. He was assigned to write a column for the *Herald Tribune* based on firsthand observations of military briefings, troop movements, the morale of Allied soldiers, and any other aspect of the war that Steinbeck felt was relevant. Steinbeck arrived in London and spent several weeks reporting on military activity in and about the city. His real objective, however, was to cover the war in battle zones in North Africa.

Steinbeck was given a transfer to North Africa and arrived in Algiers in mid-August 1943. While stationed there he applied for an assignment to cover the invasion of Italy by General Mark Clark's Fifth Army, and he recorded the landing of Allied forces at Sicily. Steinbeck chose to accompany troops on numerous perilous combat missions. While at Salerno, Steinbeck reported his experiences with an intense and compelling vividness:

An American cargo ship hit by a German bomb explodes off the coast of Sicily. Steinbeck's coverage of the invasion of Italy and of other war zones was published in 1948 in a book titled Once There Was a War.

[The correspondent's] report will be of battle plans and tactics, of taken ground or lost ground or lost terrain, of attack and counter attack. But these are some of the things he probably really saw:

He might have seen the splash of dirt and dust that is a shell burst, and a small Italian girl in the street with her stomach blown out, and he might have seen an American soldier standing over a twitching body, crying. He probably saw dead mules, lying on their sides, reduced to a pulp. He saw wreckages of houses, with torn beds hanging like shreds out of the spilled hole in a plaster wall. There were red carts and the stalled vehicles of refugees who did not get away.[64]

Steinbeck chose to describe the war as an individual soldier would see it. His columns were written from personal observation and convey this viewpoint with accuracy and authenticity. Steinbeck often reported events while under enemy fire and in the midst of combat. His dispatches for the *Herald Tribune* record an exhausting and hazardous six-month tour of duty as a journalist through the war zones of England, Africa, and Italy. In 1948 this material was published in a book titled *Once There Was a War.*

After completing his assignment as a war correspondent, Steinbeck returned to New York in early October. The death, destruction, and violence he had witnessed during the war had taken a terrible toll. Gwyndolyn was shocked to see how physically and emotionally exhausted her husband was. Although he did not mention his condition to her, Steinbeck had had both his eardrums burst by the heavy bombardment from German artillery at the Salerno beachhead and also suffered from intense headaches, periodic blackouts, and temporary loss of memory.

Steinbeck's physical recovery was slow, and memories of the horror and heroism

Fond Visions of the Future

"You know it's a funny thing—I've written myself out of my lowness in this letter. I feel better and clearer. . . . The sun has come out on the snowy roofs and there's a barrel organ playing in the street. Maybe there's some gaiety in the world. That need have nothing to do with comfort. But I'm more patient than when I started writing this letter.

After the war is done, if I can, I know what I want if my domestic difficulties and my finances will permit it. I want about ten acres near the ocean and near Monterey and I want a shabby comfortable house and room for animals, maybe a horse, and some dogs and I want some babies. Maybe I can't ever get that but it's what I want. And I'm pretty sure that it's what Gwyn wants too."

he had seen in the war would remain with him for the rest of his life. In later years Steinbeck developed a philosophical perspective of his experiences in World War II, which he expressed in the introduction to *Once There Was a War:*

> This war that I speak of came after the plate armor and longbows of Crecy and Agincourt and just before the little spitting experimental atom bombs of Hiroshima and Nagasaki. [These accounts] are period pieces, the attitudes archaic, the impulses romantic, and in the light of everything that has happened since, perhaps the whole body of work untrue and warped and one-sided. The pieces in this volume were written under pressure and in tension. They are as real as the wicked witch and the good fairy, as true and tested and edited as any other myth.[65]

The tested "myths" of battle in Steinbeck's combat experiences were to deeply affect his future writing. The bloodshed and suffering he witnessed had compelled him to test his own courage and had validated the integrity of his patriotism. Since early youth Steinbeck's writing had been influenced by personal beliefs in courage, honor, and the persistent conflict of good against evil. The crucible of combat had tested and strengthened these convictions for Steinbeck, and the themes would be dramatized in many of the books he would write in the years that followed.

6 Return to California

Steinbeck returned from his wartime duty in Europe with a renewed love of both his country and his birthplace. During the war, Steinbeck had greatly missed his family and friends. While still waiting to receive his journalism assignment overseas, he had often thought nostalgically about

As he recovered from his traumatic war experiences, Steinbeck became determined to explore new directions with his writing.

the town of Monterey. In May 1943, he had written to Webster Street:

> All last week I had a strong nostalgia for the Peninsula. Got to dreaming about it. I wish I could go back. . . . I hope when [the war] is over that I'll have a little money left so I can go back to [Pacific] Grove and spend a couple of years on a book I want to write.[66]

As Steinbeck recovered from his war experiences, he reflected on his personal need to discover meaningful new directions for his writing. The search for these new literary directions was to eventually compel Steinbeck to return to California. This homecoming proved in many ways to be a disappointment. During this time, however, Steinbeck produced some of his finest novellas, including a series of tales that were destined to make a legend out of a Monterey waterfront.

After completing his tour of duty as a war correspondent, Steinbeck turned his attention once again to writing the book he had mentioned in the letter to Street. Steinbeck was still suffering from exhaustion, however, and progress on the book was slow. Deciding that they needed a change of scenery, Steinbeck and Gwyndolyn departed for Mexico on January 11, 1944, where he planned to continue working on a new novel he had begun about a community of people living near Monterey. The two-month vacation provided Steinbeck with a much-needed rest, as he described in a letter to his editor, Pascal Covici:

> We have been doing completely tourist things and I haven't wanted to do any writing. I'll get to work on the little book as soon as I get back. It is being a good rest here in a way and a mulling over of a lot of things. I'm doing more mulling than anything else.
>
> This is a new pen and I like it very much. I got it to finish the little book with because it is good for drawing. . . . Also I have some new characters. I could sit down and do the book now, but I want to let it mellow a little longer. Meanwhile I think of it a great deal.
>
> The food is good here and I am sleeping many hours at a time—almost like a drugged sleep. Seem to have been more tired than I knew.[67]

Legend and Lore of a California Waterfront

The "little book" to which Steinbeck referred in his letter to Covici was *Cannery Row*, and it would become his next published novel. During this period, Steinbeck had also begun developing another book based on a folk tale about an Indian boy who finds a large and precious pearl.

While in Mexico, Steinbeck learned that his wife Gwyn was expecting their first child. The Steinbecks returned to New York in March 1944, where Steinbeck continued to write. "I have been working madly at a book [*Cannery Row*] and Gwyn has been working calmly at a baby and it looks as it might be a photo finish. That should be a good omen if you like omens,"[68] Steinbeck wrote to Webster Street on July 4, 1944. On August 2, 1944, Gwyndolyn gave birth to their first son whom the couple named Thom.

In the fall of 1944, Steinbeck moved his family to California and settled in a large adobe house he had purchased in Monterey. His work on *Cannery Row* continued to proceed smoothly, as he reported in a letter to Carlton Sheffield in September 1944:

> I finished the book called *Cannery Row*. It will be out in January. If Pat Covici sends me an extra proof I'll send you one. I don't know whether it is effective or not. It's written on four levels and people can take what they can receive out of it. One thing—it never mentions the war—not once. I would be anxious to know what you think of it. You'll find a lot of things in it. I find I go back to extensions of things we talked about years ago.[69]

Cannery Row is a humorous, nostalgic story of the colorful waterfront community of the same name located in Monterey, California. In writing *Cannery Row*, Steinbeck drew from his own experiences, recalling the hungry and hopeful times he had shared with friends on the Monterey waterfront during his struggling years as a writer. Most prominent among these companions was Steinbeck's best friend Ed Ricketts, who provided the inspiration for Doc, the main character in *Cannery Row*.

Steinbeck opens his novel with a graphic description of the community that

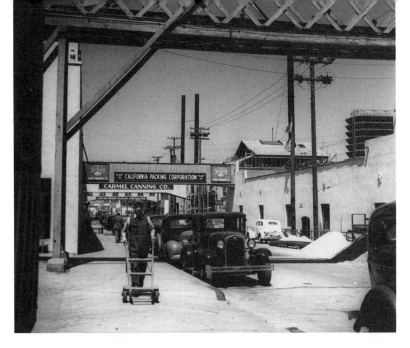

As a struggling writer in the 1930s Steinbeck had spent a great deal of time in the colorful waterfront district of Cannery Row. His nostalgia for the community and its people would be portrayed in his novel Cannery Row.

conveys the author's intimate knowledge and love of the district and its people:

> Cannery Row in Monterey in California is a poem, a stink, a grating noise, a quality of light, a tone, a habit, a nostalgia, a dream. Cannery Row is the gathered and scattered, tin and iron and rust and splintered wood, chipped pavement and weedy lots and junk heaps, sardine canneries of corrugated iron, honky tonks, restaurants and whore houses, and little crowded groceries, and laboratories and flophouses. Its inhabitants are, as the man once said, "whores, pimps, gamblers, and sons of bitches," by which he meant Everybody. Had the man looked through another peephole he might have said, "Saints and angels and martyrs and holy men," and he would have meant the same thing.[70]

Cannery Row relates the adventures of Doc and his friends, including Mack and the boys and Flora and her girls. One of the major themes in *Cannery Row* is the ecological philosophy that Steinbeck wrote about in *The Log from "The Sea of Cortez"*: that all living creatures are interrelated. The community of friends described in *Cannery Row* is to the author a microcosm of the world itself, where every living creature is regarded as a unit of a larger and collective organism or intelligence.

Steinbeck described *Cannery Row* in a letter to his friend Ritchie Lovejoy: "All fiction of course but born of homesickness. And there are some true incidents in it."[71] Steinbeck examines the process of life and death through the experiences of characters he has created from personal memories. The ultimate philosophy that Steinbeck strove to convey in *Cannery Row* was that love and beauty, which bring joy to the act of living, are the most meaningful things in life.

Cannery Row was published in 1945 and received mixed reviews. Because of its focus on impoverished people living on the fringe of society, certain reviewers dismissed it as an imitation of Steinbeck's earlier novel, *Tortilla Flat*. Despite this critical disapproval, *Cannery Row* was well received by the public and generated enormous sales.

A Disappointing Homecoming

Following the publication of *Cannery Row*, Steinbeck continued work on his next novel, *The Pearl*, which he described in a letter to Elizabeth Otis as "a strange piece of work, full of curious methods and figures. A folk tale I hope. A black-white story like a parable."[72] *The Pearl* relates the story of a poor fisherman named Kino who finds a fabulous pearl, which at first seems to promise wealth and a bright future to Kino, his wife Juana, and their infant son Coyotito. The little family undertakes a journey to sell the pearl, and they eventually come to realize that the gem, which leads them to tragedy, is a symbol of evil and greed.

Since the publication of *The Grapes of Wrath*, Steinbeck had become one of the most famous writers in America and en-

---

"The Lovely Colored World"

In Cannery Row, *Steinbeck described the Monterey waterfront district as a little society similar to a Pacific tide pool. Steinbeck regarded both microcosms as examples of ecological communities, having similar life cycles and interrelated with all other units of nature.*

"Doc was collecting marine animals in the Great Tide Pool on the tip of the Peninsula. It is a fabulous place: when the tide is in, a wave-churned basin, creamy with foam, whipped by the combers that roll in from the whistling buoy on the reef. But when the tide goes out the little water world becomes quiet and lovely. The sea is very clear and the bottom becomes fantastic with hurrying, fighting, feeding, breeding animals. Crabs rush from frond to frond of the waving algae. Starfish squat over mussels and limpets, attach their million little suckers and then slowly lift with incredible power until the prey is broken from the rock. And then the starfish stomach comes out and envelops its food. Orange and speckled and fluted nudibranchs [shell-less mollusks] slide gracefully over the rocks, their skirts waving like the dresses of Spanish dancers. And black eels poke their heads out of crevices and wait for prey. The snapping shrimps with their trigger claws pop loudly. The lovely colored world is glassed over."

An Omen of Evil

Steinbeck wrote The Pearl *as an allegory of good and evil. The novel is a fable about a young fisherman named Kino who finds a fabulous pearl, which comes to symbolize greed and evil.*

"He looked into his pearl to find his vision. 'When we sell it at last, I will have a rifle,' he said, and he looked into the shining surface for his rifle, but he saw only a huddled dark body on the ground with shining blood dripping from its throat. And he said quickly, 'We will be married in a great church.' And in the pearl he saw Juana with her beaten face crawling home through the night. 'Our son must learn to read,' he said frantically. And there in the pearl [was] Coyotito's face, thick and feverish from the medicine.

And Kino thrust the pearl back into his clothing, and the music of the pearl had become sinister in his ears, and it was interwoven with the music of evil."

Kino (with son in lap) gathers with friends and family in this still from the movie version of The Pearl.

joyed a wide and loyal following of readers. *The Pearl* was published in 1947 and proved to be an excellent seller. In addition Steinbeck had agreed to write a script and work with a film company in Mexico to produce *The Pearl* as a motion picture. Arrangements were made for the Steinbecks to return to Mexico in the spring and Gwyn would assist in the musical scoring of the film by gathering and transcribing regional folk themes.

In April 1945, the Steinbecks arrived in Cuernavaca, Mexico, where they rented a spacious house with a lovely garden and large swimming pool. Steinbeck began work on another book, which he decided to title *The Wayward Bus*. The vacation in Mexico also provided Steinbeck with an opportunity to absent himself from Monterey, California, and to reassess his feelings about continuing to live there.

Steinbeck's California homecoming had not been entirely successful. While still in New York, he had hoped for a happy reunion with old friends and acquaintances. Upon his return to California, however, he found that many of the people he had once known were envious of his great success and fame. Among these people were certain friends to whom Steinbeck had over the years provided financial support and personal encouragement.

One of the people with whom he was particularly disappointed was a longtime friend named Ritchie Lovejoy. When Steinbeck won the Pulitzer Prize in 1940, he had given the $1,000 prize money to Lovejoy, who was writing a novel himself and was able to use the cash to live on. When Steinbeck returned to Monterey in 1944, however, Lovejoy was working at a small town newspaper and had still not completed his novel.

A disagreement between the two men arose when Steinbeck was offered an assignment to write an article on Cannery Row for *Life* magazine. Steinbeck refused, believing that such an article would intrude on the privacy of friends, including Ed Ricketts, still living in the community. When Lovejoy learned of Steinbeck's refusal, he applied to *Life* offering to write the article and had received the job.

Steinbeck was angered by Lovejoy's acceptance of the magazine assignment and considered it to be a betrayal of himself and all the people on Cannery Row. In Steinbeck's estimation, Lovejoy was a failed writer who was willing to sell out his friends for money. His disgust over the matter was expressed in a letter to Elizabeth Otis:

> Ritch has us by the whatyoucallems because he needs money. It's funny because he would be the first to blame me if I did it. But of course if *Life* wanted to do it they could anyway. I don't know why they are so insistent. . . . Clever trick of theirs, wasn't it? Ed [Ricketts] wouldn't have consented for any other reason than to help Ritchie. So there it is. . . . But Ritchie has an invariable method. When he thinks he has the sale he raises the price. And he may ask so much that they will give the whole thing up. *One's friends!* How he would have sneered if I did it. And that's that.[73]

Steinbeck takes time out from the filming of The Pearl *in Cuernavaca, Mexico, to play in the pool with Gwyn and his son Thom.*

Steinbeck had hoped that when he returned to California, he would be able to escape the public attention and professional pressures he had experienced in New York. He planned to resettle in his hometown, where he believed his neighbors would accept him as simply another ordinary member of the community. Steinbeck found instead that he was pursued as a celebrity by curious citizens in Monterey, just as he had been in New York.

Steinbeck was depressed over the resentful attitudes expressed by such old friends as Lovejoy. Among them all, he felt that only Ed Ricketts remained unchanged in his affection and loyalty. Steinbeck found it difficult to understand that the tremendous fame he had achieved as a writer would make it impossible for him to resume the simple, anonymous life he had enjoyed in Monterey many years before.

Birth of a New Project

During his stay in Cuernavaca, Steinbeck wrote his theatrical agent Annie Laurie Williams a letter informing her that he was considering writing a screenplay on Emiliano Zapata, the legendary leader of the Mexican revolution.

There is a thing I want to discuss with you. I was approached the other day by an outfit that calls itself Pan American Films with the proposition that I do a film on the life of Emiliano Zapata. Now there is no other story I would rather do. But there are certain things in the way.

I have, as you know, work ahead for a long time to come. I would not even be ready to make a start until a year from this fall.

A Strange Phenomenon

Throughout his life Steinbeck possessed a sense of mysticism. A vivid example of his identification with the supernatural is found in this letter to Pascal Covici, written in Cuernavaca and found in Steinbeck: a Life in Letters.

"Last night a very strange thing happened. Anciently it would have had a very definite effect on a person. The moon came up red and sullen through a black haze. We sat on the porch watching it because of its very threatening color. These black clouds like mares' tails moved up from the horizon, big black streaks. Jack Wagner yelled suddenly—'Look!' It was a very strange thing. The clouds spelled in huge black letters JOHN right across the moon. It was very definite and lasted five minutes before it drifted away. We called Gwyn to look at it. I have seen letters in clouds before but never four definite letters. In an age of portents [omens] it would be effective. Such a thing might have caused the Magna Carta not to be signed."

Steinbeck spent two years doing research for a movie about the life of Emiliano Zapata, the legendary leader of the Mexican revolution.

New York Again

Steinbeck decided that he and his family would return to New York to live when he had completed his work on the film version of *The Pearl*. He arranged to purchase two brownstone houses in New York and planned to live with his family in one and rent out the second. The Steinbecks arrived in New York City in December 1945. After living briefly in an apartment, they moved into a brownstone house on East Seventy-eighth Street.

On June 12, 1946, Gwyndolyn gave birth to their second son. "The new baby," announced Steinbeck happily to his friend Jack Wagner, "will be named John and is already called Juanito."[75] Despite his joy over the birth of their second child, Steinbeck's second marriage had become increasingly unhappy. Gwyn resented Steinbeck's constant traveling and frequent absences from home. She felt neglected and complained frequently that her husband was preventing her from achieving professional success on her own as a writer and singer.

Steinbeck in turn felt that Gwyn's lack of professional drive had prevented her from having a successful career. The conflicts between them continued to grow. In a letter written to his friend Bo Beskow on December 16, 1946, Steinbeck confided that he and his wife had separated:

> I think Gwyn and the children will go to California for a month or six weeks about the first of February to let the children see her relatives. But I will just stay here and get back to work. Marital vacations are sometimes good things.[76]

Steinbeck's novel *The Pearl* was published in 1947 and released as a motion

The difficulty of making it straight would be very great. There are still men living and in power who helped to trick and murder Zapata. I would only make it straight. I would require gov't assurance that it could be made straight historically. This will have to be an iron bound agreement because Zapata could be one of the great films of all times as by a twist or a concession, it could be a complete double cross of the things Zapata lived and died for.[74]

Steinbeck's concern over possible interference by the Mexican government with the film caused him to decline the offer from Pan American Films. He decided instead to work independently on a script outline and would extensively research Zapata's life over the next two years.

picture in the same year. Steinbeck's friend and editor, Pat Covici, regarded *The Pearl* as an artistic success and wrote Steinbeck a letter praising the novel:

> I just finished "La Perla" and I like it. . . . In this parable you say there are only black and white things and no one in between, but what rich blacks and what dazzling whites. . . . One could also say . . . it has only three notes—love, hunger, and freedom from greed. But again what infinite longings you put into them.[77]

Heartbreak and Tragedy

In the same year, 1947, Steinbeck also published *The Wayward Bus* which he had begun writing during his visit to Cuernavaca two years earlier. Set in California, *The Wayward Bus* is an amusing account of the adventures of a busload of passengers, each of whom is embarked on a pilgrimage.

Throughout this time, Steinbeck's marriage to Gwyndolyn went from bad to worse. In an effort to reconcile their differences, the couple traveled to France in the summer of 1947. Steinbeck had accepted an assignment for the *New York Tribune* to write a series of travel articles to be focused largely on observations he would make while visiting Russia. Gwyndolyn accompanied her husband to Paris, and after a stay of several weeks there returned home, while Steinbeck went on to what was then the Soviet Union.

Steinbeck spent several weeks touring the Soviet Union, accompanied by Robert Capa, the prominent photojournalist. The two men visited Moscow, Georgia, Prague, and Budapest. The articles Steinbeck relayed to the *New York Tribune* were filled with his observations on the variety of cultures and customs encountered throughout the country.

Steinbeck and Capa completed their assignment abroad and returned to New York in October 1947. During their tour

John and Gwyn in Sweden in 1946, just prior to their separation. Despite attempts at reconciliation, the couple divorced in 1948.

"A Cosmic Bus"

While in Cuernavaca, Steinbeck's fondness for the Mexican people impelled him to begin a book called The Wayward Bus. *Included in* Steinbeck: A Life in Letters *is a letter to Pascal Covici describing the characteristic excitement Steinbeck felt about beginning a new literary project.*

"The people down here are very kind to us. And I hope out of this stay to write a book that may be something for them to have. For the Wayward Bus could be something like the Don Quixote of Mexico. The more I think of it the better I like it and the better I like it the longer its plan and the wider its scope until it seems to contain the whole ambitious thing I have ever attempted. Not that it still won't be funny but funny as Tom Jones and Tristram Shandy and Don Quixote are funny. And it isn't going to take a little time to write but a long time and I don't care for my bus is something large in my mind. It is a cosmic bus holding sparks and back firing into the Milky Way and turning the corner of Betelgeuse [a giant red star] without a hand signal. And Juan Chicoy [the driver in *The Wayward Bus*] is all the god the fathers you ever saw driving a six cylinder broken down, battered world through time and space. If I can do it well *The Wayward Bus* will be a pleasant thing."

in Russia, Steinbeck had begun considering an idea for a new book, which he confided in a letter to Webster Street:

I have a great deal of work to do this year and I would like to get it all done by this summer because then I would like to stop everything to do a long novel that I have been working on the notes of for a long time. It seems to me that for the last few years I have been working on bits and pieces of things without much continuity and I want to get back to a long slow piece of work. I need to go out there for a lot of research so I may be out in California this summer. I'd be glad if I could for a little while. I'm living too hectic a life but then so are you and so is everyone.[78]

Steinbeck was also looking forward to taking another scientific research trip with Ed Ricketts. The two friends hoped to travel to Canadian waters—to the Queen Charlotte Islands off the coast of British Columbia, where Steinbeck and Ricketts planned to collaborate on another book, to be titled *The Outer Shores*. Steinbeck looked forward to a reunion with Ricketts and was excited over the prospect of working with him again.

While in the midst of preparing for his return to California, Steinbeck was stunned to learn that Ricketts had been critically injured in an automobile accident. Frantic with worry and grief, Steinbeck rushed to book a flight to California. He arrived in Salinas, on May 11, 1948, to learn that Ed had died earlier that day.

Steinbeck reacted to Ricketts's death with intense sorrow. He had known Ed Ricketts for eighteen years and considered him to be his best friend. Ricketts had been both confidant and mentor throughout Steinbeck's writing career. A few days after Ricketts's death, Steinbeck wrote to his friend Bo Beskow:

> I got back from Monterey to find your letter. You see, Ed Ricketts' car was hit by a train and after fighting for his life for three days he died, and there died the greatest man I have known and the best teacher. It is going to take a long time to reorganize my thinking and my planning without him. It is good that he was killed during the very best time of his life with his work at its peak and with the best girl he ever had. I am extremely glad for that.[79]

Steinbeck's rise to success as an author had brought many changes in his life. He had achieved literary honors, public acclaim, and financial wealth, but he had also endured the death of his parents, divorce from his first wife, and the envy and jealousy of numerous friends.

The death of Ed Ricketts, however, was a particularly devastating blow. The mild-mannered, scholarly scientist had been Steinbeck's strongest ally and closest friend. He had spent countless hours discussing scientific and philosophical theories with the marine biologist while drinking wine or listening to selections of the classical music Ricketts loved. The two friends had explored tide pools together, and they shared a fascination with natural ecology. They had planned to record the results of their scientific research in books that Steinbeck now knew would never be written.

The funeral service held for Ed Ricketts was attended by only a few people. Unlike Steinbeck, Ricketts was not famous at the time of his death. Since his passing, however, countless readers have come to know Ed Ricketts through the characters he inspired in John Steinbeck's books.

Steinbeck had always turned to writing as a way of seeking solace from the tragedies in his life. A few days after Ricketts's funeral, Steinbeck wrote a letter to Ritch and Tal Lovejoy in which he expressed some thoughts about the great impact Ed's death had had on him. Despite his grief, Steinbeck closed this letter by declaring a new resolve to continue his writing:

> Nothing about me is the same. It is all changed. Tightening up now but in a kind of different way. Almost a relief to be alone. As though some kind of conscience were removed and a fierceness I haven't had for many years restored. I'm going to work now as I have never worked before, because for the time being anyway, that's all there is.[80]

Chapter

7 Turbulent Years

The death of Ed Ricketts ended an eighteen-year friendship that had in many ways encompassed one of the happiest and most eventful periods in Steinbeck's life. During those years, too, the writer had been saddened by the death of his parents and his divorce from Carol and had endured severe hardship as a war correspondent in Europe and Africa. After attending Ed Ricketts's funeral, Steinbeck prepared to return to New York, determined to continue his writing career with even greater intensity, unaware that he was about to enter one of the most turbulent periods of his life.

Upon his arrival home Gwyndolyn confronted him with the news that she wanted a divorce, informing Steinbeck that she was no longer in love with him and had not loved him for years. Despite their many bitter disagreements, Steinbeck had hoped that the marriage could be saved, but his wife's announcement ended all thought of a reconciliation. Steinbeck confided the unhappy news to Bo Beskow in a letter indicating that he had resigned himself to the divorce:

After four years of bitter unhappiness Gwyn has decided that she wants a divorce. It is an old story of female frustration. She wants something I can't give her so she must go on looking. And maybe she will never find out that no one can give it to her. But that is her business now. She has cut me off completely. She will take the children, at least for the time being. And I will go back to Monterey to try to get rest-

Following his divorce and the death of his close friend Ed Ricketts, Steinbeck entered one of the darkest periods of his life.

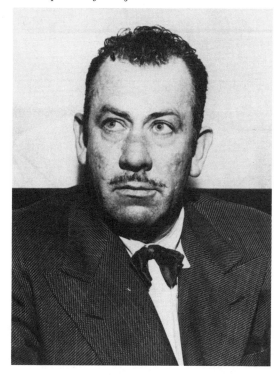

ed and get the smell of my own country again. She did one kind thing. She killed my love of her with little cruelties so there is not much shock in all of this. And I will come back. I'm pretty sure I have some material left. But I have to rest like an old dog fox-panting beside a stream. I have great sadness but no anger. In Pacific Grove I have the little cottage my father built and I will live and work in it for a while. Maybe I'll come to see you next winter and we'll "sing sad stories of the death of kings"—with herring.[81]

Steinbeck's divorce from Gwyn was one of the darkest periods of his life. Still grief-stricken over the death of Ed Ricketts, Steinbeck was nearly overwhelmed with sorrow over the failure of his second marriage. On September 1, 1948, he returned to his family house in Pacific Grove. Steinbeck had brought with him little more than the clothes on his back because he had been compelled to forfeit most of his property and financial assets in the divorce settlement.

Struggle for Survival

Steinbeck was nearly destitute. The divorce proceedings had exhausted his savings, and he owed money to the government for taxes. Despite the commercial success of his books, the incoming royalties would not be enough for the alimony and child support he was now obligated to pay.

For the first time in many years, Steinbeck was faced with the necessity of writing for the specific intention of earning money. Editor and close friend Pascal Covici sympathized with this dilemma and loyally continued to encourage Steinbeck's literary endeavors as the writer struggled to rebuild his life. Covici felt that many of

Parental Philosophy

Steinbeck made great efforts to maintain a close relationship with his sons, John Jr. and Thom. An excerpt from this letter to Elaine Scott, included in Steinbeck: A Life in Letters, *reveals the author's deep affection for his sons.*

"Thom needs a pet so badly and today one of his friends offered him a kitten and he wants it so dreadfully. He brought it up very casually and offhand—and kind of deadly. I mean in a dead manner as though he knew I would refuse to let him have it. His mother had refused. And he really needs it. And I had to make a judgment. The richness of having the kitten against the heartbreak of not being able to take it to New York with him. In the morning if he wants it, he can have it even if he does have to give it up. To refuse him would be like refusing love because you might get hurt and that's the best I can do."

Steinbeck's personal and financial problems had resulted from various people who had taken advantage of his generosity over the years. In a letter written to Steinbeck in September 1948, Covici offered a brief analysis of the roots of Steinbeck's suffering and also revealed a friend's insight into Steinbeck's character:

> It is difficult to get rid of poison which has permeated your whole body and mind for so long. You could never say "No" to any second-rater who forced himself upon you. . . . By nature shy and retiring and almost uncommunicative, you never would go out of your way to meet the people of your choice, but the second-raters, who never wait, forced themselves on you and you, being also very compassionate and human, made easy companions of them when at heart you really didn't want them and much preferred to be alone.[82]

Steinbeck spent the first six weeks of his return to Pacific Grove repairing the house and restoring the garden. He found that the physical labor required to do this work brought him welcome relief from brooding over his personal difficulties. Because of Steinbeck's extreme financial situation, Covici had sent a supply of yellow tablets so that Steinbeck could continue his writing.

A Desperate Resolution to Write

Steinbeck was deeply committed to completing the screenplay he had begun two years earlier on the life of Emiliano Zapata. In 1948 Steinbeck had accepted a proposal from Darryl F. Zanuck, the head of Twentieth-Century Fox Studios, to write a film script for a motion picture to be titled *Viva Zapata!* Steinbeck's work on the script had proceeded slowly in Pacific Grove as he battled depression over his divorce from Gwyn and the death of Ed Ricketts. For the first time in his life, Steinbeck found it difficult and at times nearly impossible to write.

Pascal Covici and other close friends grew alarmed over Steinbeck's despondence. In November 1948, Mildred Lyman, a representative from the literary agency of McIntosh & Otis, visited Steinbeck and wrote a troubled letter to her colleague Annie Laurie Williams:

> He is deeply disturbed and frightened about his work. . . . The fact that so much time has elapsed without his accomplishing anything to speak of worries him a great deal. He has a defense mechanism which is constantly in action and it is hard to get behind that. What John needs more than anything right now is discipline.[83]

Steinbeck continued to struggle with writing the screenplay for *Viva Zapata!* as well as a novelette in play form called *Burning Bright*, which was published as a book and produced as a Broadway play in 1950. Although Steinbeck still had financial difficulties, his contract with Zanuck to write the Zapata script was providing an income, and he had begun to grow excited about the project. In a letter written to Bo Beskow in the winter of 1948, Steinbeck indicated that his spirit and literary ambition had begun to revive:

> In the morning I awaken to see the sun on my little garden and a flood of joy comes over me—such a thing I have not felt for many years. My material for

the Zapata script is all collected now and next Monday I will go to work on it with great energy, for I have great energy again. But the churning joy in the guts that to me is the physical symptom of creation is there again.[84]

By the spring of 1949, Steinbeck had completed a draft of the Zapata script and Zanuck assigned a producer from the studio named Jules Buck to assist Steinbeck with the dialogue for the screenplay. The two men worked together for a month at Steinbeck's house developing the script. Buck was impressed by Steinbeck's professionalism and later recalled the author's diligent efforts to perfect the script:

He [Steinbeck] would write in this very meticulous closed handwriting, and he would dictate into a recording machine and listen to a playback. "No, that's not right," and he would do something and then he would say, "How does this sound?" (And I would say) "Wonderful, great," whatever, you know, or "No John, try it again." But anyway, he would always come up with something that, you know, really sparked. Or he would take an idea and say, "No, that's no good, but you gave me something else that I can use.". . . If he didn't understand something in his own mind, he'd say, "Wait a minute, I want to draw how the scene should be played."[85]

The screenplay for *Viva Zapata!* was completed in 1951 and the motion picture,

---

"We'll Make It Perfect"

Although written during the difficult period following his divorce from Gwyndolyn, Steinbeck's script for the motion picture Viva Zapata! *became a moving and eloquent screenplay. Included in* Steinbeck: A Life in Letters *is this letter to the film's director, Elia Kazan.*

"Last night Elaine read me parts of the script. She liked it very much and I must say I did too. It is a little double action jewel of a script. But I was glad to hear it again because before it is mouthed by actors, I want to go over the dialogue once more for very small changes. Things like—'For that matter.' 'As a matter of fact'—in other words all filler wants to come out. There isn't much but there is some. I'll want no word in dialogue that has not some definite reference to the story. You once said that you would like this to be a kind of monument. By the same token I would like it to be as tight and terse as possible. It is awfully good but it can be better. Just dialogue—I heard a dozen places where I can clean it and sharpen it. But outside of that I am very much pleased with it. I truly believe it is a classic example of good film writing. So we'll make it perfect."

Steinbeck's screenplay, Viva Zapata!, *became a motion picture in 1951. The movie, a huge box office success, starred Marlon Brando (right) as Emiliano Zapata.*

released in the same year, produced impressive box office sales. Steinbeck's collaboration with Buck resulted in a character study of Emiliano Zapata that was compelling and forceful. In the motion picture, Zapata is a brooding figure who emerges from the turbulent background of a political revolution to become the heroic military leader of Mexican peasants in their fight against government oppression. Much of Steinbeck's affinity toward the Mexican people, evident in some of his earlier works like *Tortilla Flat*, is again seen in his admiring dramatic depiction of Zapata.

Romance and Elaine

One of the major reasons for Steinbeck's renewed vigor in his writing was his growing friendship with an actress named Elaine Scott, whom Steinbeck had met in the summer of 1949. Despite a bitter distrust of women resulting from his divorce from Gwyndolyn, Steinbeck found himself attracted to Elaine, who was separated from actor Zachary Scott.

Upon the finalization of her divorce from Scott, Elaine and Steinbeck were married in a formal ceremony at the home of Steinbeck's publisher on December 28, 1950. Steinbeck's marriage to Elaine, which lasted until his death in 1968, brought him the greatest sense of peace and happiness he had ever known. In a letter to his friends Jack and Max Wagner, Steinbeck confided his deep affection for Elaine:

> I guess it isn't that Elaine gets better all the time but rather that I knowing her better am able to see more and more of her goodnesses. She is the best girl I ever knew.[86]

John and Elaine at their wedding reception in 1950. The couple remained happily married until his death in 1968.

A Lifetime Literary Ambition

Upon returning from their honeymoon in Bermuda, the Steinbecks moved into a house they had purchased on East Seventy-Second Street in New York City. Although the couple found it necessary to maintain a cautious budget, Steinbeck's financial situation had improved considerably and he felt a greater encouragement over his writing prospects. Steinbeck was anxious to begin work on the "long novel," he had mentioned earlier in a letter to Webster Street. Originally titled *The Salinas Valley*, the novel was to be a lengthy book based on the history of Steinbeck's own family. To Steinbeck, it would be the most ambitious work of his career.

"Of course I want the new book to be good," Steinbeck declared in a letter to George Albee with whom he had reconciled:

> I have wanted all of them to be good. But with the others—all of them—I had a personal out. I could—say—it is just really practice for "the book." If you can't do this one, the practice was not worth it. So you see I feel at once stimulated and scared. The terror of starting is invariable but I am more terrified not knowing more about technique than I did.[87]

Steinbeck decided to keep a journal recording the daily progress of his new novel, which he began writing in February 1951, under a new title, *East of Eden*. Many of the journal entries were composed in the form of letters addressed to his editor Pascal Covici. In these letters, Steinbeck often described the various challenges he encountered in writing *East of Eden*. In an initial letter, which became the book's foreword, Steinbeck stated his intention of dedicating *East of Eden* to his two sons, Thom and John:

> I am choosing to write this book to my sons. They are little boys now and they will never know what they came from through me, unless I tell them. It is not written for them to read now but when they are grown and the pains and joys have touseled them a little. . . . One can go off into fanciness if one writes to a huge nebulous group but I think it will be necessary to speak very straight and clearly and simply if I

Radiant Recollections of Home

Many of Steinbeck's boyhood memories of the Salinas Valley were described in vibrant detail in East of Eden. *His vivid recollection of the beautiful wildflowers of the region was a striking example of the poetic lyricism that characterized much of Steinbeck's writing.*

"The spring flowers in a wet year were unbelievable. The whole valley floor and the foothills too, would be carpeted with lupins and poppies. Once a woman told me that colored flowers would seem more bright if you added a few white flowers to give the colours definition. Every petal of blue lupin is edged with white, so that a field of lupins is more blue than you can imagine. And mixed with these were splashes of California poppies. These too are a burning colour—not orange, not gold, but if pure gold were liquid and could raise a cream, that golden cream might be like the colour of the poppies. When their season was over the yellow mustard came up and grew to a great height. When my grandfather came into the valley, the mustard was so tall that a man on horseback showed only his head above the yellow flowers. On the uplands the grass would be strewn with buttercups, with hen-and-chickens, with black-centered yellow violets. And a little later in the season there would be the red and yellow stands of Indian paintbrush. These were the flowers of the open spaces exposed to the sun."

Steinbeck dedicated East of Eden *to his two sons Thom and John.*

address my book to two little boys who will be men before they read my book. They have no great background of the world of literature, they don't know the great stories of the world as we do.

And so I will tell them one of the greatest, perhaps the greatest story of all—the story of good and evil, of strength and weakness, of love and hate, of beauty and ugliness.[88]

East of Eden is set in the Salinas Valley and relates the saga of the Hamilton and Trask families, which spans three generations. Steinbeck drew heavily on his own family history in writing this novel and painstakingly researched the regional history of Salinas.

Journal of a Novel

Steinbeck worked intensely throughout 1952, writing *East of Eden* and faithfully recording the book's evolution in his journal. In reality he was writing two books. One was the novel itself, and the other one was a volume describing the creation

To Steinbeck, the writing of East of Eden *(on display in foreground) represented the pinnacle of his writing career. Unfortunately, the book fell short of Steinbeck's high expectations for it.*

of a novel. Viking Press published the second book in 1969, a year after Steinbeck's death, under the title *Journal of a Novel: The "East of Eden" Letters.*

In this journal, Steinbeck expressed some of his most candid and personal thoughts and beliefs about writing. The writing of *East of Eden* represented to Steinbeck the summit of his writing career. The journal relates an absorbing account of the discipline, challenges, despair, and elation that Steinbeck faced in the nearly year-long struggle to achieve what he hoped would be his highest literary achievement. Many of the entries present fascinating insights on how Steinbeck felt about being a writer.

> August 22: It is quite early. Elaine is going to take the boys to a movie this afternoon and then they are coming back and we are all going out to dinner. So I have all day at my desk and I like that. I feel so good today—just wonderful. I have a kind of soaring joyousness.

> August 24: Suddenly I feel lonely in a curious kind of way. I guess I am afraid. That always comes near the end of a book—the fear that you have not accomplished what you started to do.

> September 6: As to the work itself, only time will show whether it has been good. Sometimes it seems to me actually to have the high purpose I set for it, and at other times it seems pedestrian and trite. I know how much work must go into it after it is done but I have plenty of time for that and I am quite willing to do it. This is *the* Book as far as I am concerned.[89]

East of Eden was published in 1952 and by November had become a number one

A Professional Tribute

Steinbeck's close association with his editor Pascal Covici deepened during the writing of East of Eden. *Included in* Steinbeck: A Life in Letters *is this excerpt from the letter in which Steinbeck informed his editor that the book would be dedicated to him.*

"I have decided for this, my book, *East of Eden,* to write dedication, prologue, argument, apology and perhaps epitaph all in one.

The dedication is to you with all the admiration and affection that have been distilled from our singularly blessed association of many years. This book is inscribed to you because you have been part of its birth and growth.

As you know, a prologue is written last but placed first to explain the book's shortcomings and to ask the reader to be kind. But a prologue is also a note of farewell from the writer to his book. For years the writer and his book have been together—friends or bitter enemies but very close as only love and fighting can accomplish.

Then suddenly the book is done. It is a kind of death. This is the requiem."

best-seller, but in many ways the novel fell short of Steinbeck's hopes. *East of Eden* is a stirring and heroic epic, but it is flawed in many ways with respect to plot, and various critics found the use of dialogue to be at times dated and awkward. Steinbeck was undismayed. At the age of fifty he had philosophically concluded that artistic perfection was an impossibility that a writer must nevertheless still strive to achieve. In the initial letter written for *Journal of a Novel: The "East of Eden" Letters,* Steinbeck reaffirmed his creed as a writer.

In utter loneliness a writer tries to explain the inexplicable. And sometimes if he is very fortunate and if the time is right, a very little of what he is trying to do trickles through—not very much. And if he is a writer wise enough to know that it can't be done, then he is not a writer at all. A good writer always works at the impossible.[90]

Steinbeck continued his quest to perfect his work until the end of his life. This persistence, he felt, was essential to the creative integrity of a true writer. Despite Steinbeck's belief that writing was a lonely and difficult profession, his aspiration to excel in literature was an ideal that he cherished and never abandoned.

8 In Search of New Challenges

In 1952 Steinbeck, at the age of fifty, was one of the most famous American authors in the world, ranking in prominence with William Faulkner and Ernest Hemingway. Steinbeck's impressive literary achievements, along with his extensive world travels and personal popularity among Hollywood celebrities, politicians, and other writers and artists, were all factors that significantly matured Steinbeck into a more socially expansive and worldly man.

After completing *East of Eden*, Steinbeck and Elaine decided to embark on an extended European vacation. Steinbeck arranged to finance the trip by writing a series of articles on his travels for *Collier's* magazine. In late March 1952, the Steinbecks departed for Europe, beginning a six-month international tour that would take them through Spain, France, Switzerland, and the British Isles. The European tour provided a welcome interval of rest for Steinbeck after the exhaustive year of work on *East of Eden*.

While traveling abroad, Steinbeck considered new directions in his writing. The articles he contributed to *Collier's* are written from a more personal viewpoint than was used in much of his earlier work. In

John and Elaine sightsee in Venice. For a respite from his exhaustive work schedule, the Steinbecks embarked on an extended European vacation.

Steinbeck attributed much of his happiness to Elaine—his wife, friend, and travel companion.

one particularly autobiographical article titled "I Go Back to Ireland," Steinbeck described with warmth and poignance the thoughts and feelings he experienced in returning to the land of his mother's ancestors in search of his family roots.

The personal nature of the *Collier's* articles both marked a distinct departure from the strictly objective writing style that generally had characterized Steinbeck's work and set the tone for his last two books, *The Winter of Our Discontent* and *Travels with Charley.* It also revealed a mellowing of Steinbeck's personality.

Although Steinbeck remained essentially shy and modest throughout his life, his self-confidence increased with his professional success. In his later years he grew less reluctant to grant interviews to journalists and tended to reveal more of his personal feelings in his written work.

Shortly after returning from Europe, Steinbeck shared some pensive thoughts in a letter to Carlton Sheffield:

> Fifty is a good age. The hair recedes, the paunch grows a little, the face—rarely inspected, looks the same to us but not to others. The little inabilities grow so gradually that we don't even know it.
>
> We had the grand tour—six months of it and I liked it very well. I'm glad to be back. We have a pretty little house here and every day is full. Very nice and time races by. When you really live in New York, it is more rural than country.[91]

Elaine's Happy Influence

Steinbeck realized that his marriage to Elaine was one of the greatest reasons for his happiness. In another letter to Sheffield, written in October 1952, Steinbeck confided that he was changed in some ways, more calm, maybe more adult, perhaps more tolerant. But still restless.

> I'll never get over that I guess—still nervous, still going from my high ups to very low downs—just short of a manic depressive, I guess. I have more confidence in myself now, which makes me less arrogant. And Elaine has taught me not to be afraid of people [strangers] so that I am kinder and better mannered I think.[92]

Steinbeck had found in Elaine a wife who understood his continual restlessness and shared his passion for travel. She also assisted her husband in his correspondent assignments by acting as his photographer.

The Novelist's Story

One of Steinbeck's most revealing letters regarding his philosophy of the novel as an art form is excerpted here from Steinbeck: A Life in Letters. *It was written from Rome, Italy, in the spring of 1957 to Elizabeth Otis and a literary colleague, Chase Horton.*

"A novelist not only puts down a story but he is the story. He is each one of the characters in a greater or a less degree. And because he is usually a moral man in intention and honest in his approach, he sets things down as truly as he can.

A novel may be said to be the man who writes it. Now it is nearly always true that a novelist, perhaps unconsciously, identifies himself with one chief or central character in his novel. Into this character he puts not only what he thinks he is but what he hopes to be. We can call this spokesman the self-character. You will find one in every one of my books and in the novels of everyone I can remember. It is most simple and near the surface in Hemingway's novels. The soldier, romantic, always maimed in some sense, hand—testicles. These are the symbols of his limitations. I suppose my own symbol character has my dream wish of wisdom and acceptance."

Steinbeck remained committed to the pursuit of artistic perfection in his writing.

Jules Buck, with whom Steinbeck had collaborated on *Viva Zapata!*, paid a visit to the Steinbecks while they were in Paris. Later he remarked on the happy influence Elaine had on her husband:

Elaine brought him out, brought out that side of him that was always trying to escape. He was bashful, and having gone through a very rough early period, a very careful man in many ways. But when things were going really well, my God the look on his face was pure happiness.[93]

A Disappointing Endeavor

Upon their return to New York, Steinbeck began work on a new book which he called *Bear Flag*. Written as a sequel to *Cannery Row*, the novel was composed with the intention of being converted into a musical comedy. In September 1953, Steinbeck reported in a letter to Elizabeth Otis that he was nearing completion of *Bear Flag*, and passed along some thoughts regarding the enjoyment he felt about the craft of writing:

> I have enjoyed writing this book, the B.F.
>
> There is a school of thought among writers which says that if you enjoy something it is automatically no good and should be thrown out. I can't agree with this. *Bear Flag* may not be much good but for what it is, I think it is all right. Also I think it makes a nice balance for the weight of *Eden*. It is kind of light and gay and astringent. It may even say some good things.
>
> I'll be sad to finish *Bear Flag*. I have really loved it. I am reluctant to start into the last two chapters. But I will. I do hope you love this book, a little self-indulgent though it may be. Try to like it.[94]

The book was published in 1954 under the title of *Sweet Thursday*, and the musical appeared in 1955 as a Broadway production called *Pipe Dream*. *Sweet Thursday* was the third Steinbeck novel to be produced as a Broadway play. Steinbeck was fascinated by the theater throughout his life and was continually striving to master the form in his writing.

Pipe Dream, produced by Richard Rodgers and Oscar Hammerstein II, opened

Steinbeck and Elia Kazan during the production of the Broadway play Burning Bright, *for which Steinbeck wrote the screenplay.*

in the fall of 1950. Steinbeck was deeply unhappy with the show and felt that the producers had failed to capture the spirit of the story. "What really is the trouble," wrote Steinbeck to Elia Kazan, "is that R. [Rodgers] and H. [Hammerstein] seem to be attracted to my kind of writing and they are temperamentally incapable of doing it [the play]."[95]

Steinbeck made several suggestions for Rodgers and Hammerstein, who refused to use any of them. Steinbeck's disappointment with *Pipe Dream* was so great that he never attempted to seriously write for the theater again.

In February 1955, the Steinbecks purchased a modest summer house on Long Island. The house stood on a sandy two-acre bluff and was located about a mile from the small village of Sag Harbor, New York. Their Long Island summer house in many ways resembled the family cottage Steinbeck had lived in at Pacific Grove, and the friendly village of Sag Harbor reminded him of the happy community he had once known in Cannery Row.

Shortly after purchasing the new summer home in Long Island, Steinbeck set about the task of making repairs and improvements. The physical work on the house was a welcome change, but after a few weeks of this activity, Steinbeck grew restless to return to his writing. Steinbeck aggressively sought challenges in his literary career and regarded every book he wrote as an opportunity to experiment with new forms in writing. Few things displeased him more than to be categorized

A Writer's Changing Fortunes

Despite the great commercial success of his books, Steinbeck suffered numerous financial setbacks during his career. These remarks, excerpted from a letter to Carlton Sheffield in Steinbeck: A Life in Letters, *reveal something of Steinbeck's attitude toward money.*

"I have never expected to make a living at writing. Then when money began to come in it kind of scared me. I didn't think I deserved it and besides it was kind of bad luck. I gave a lot of it away—tried to spread it around. Maybe it was a kind of propitiation [appeasement] of the gods. It made me a lot of enemies. I was clumsy about it I guess but I didn't want power over any one. Anyway that was the impulse. And it was wrong. But I've done many wrong things.

I don't have any money problems any more. After living and taxes and alimony, there isn't quite any left so my problem is solved. We [Steinbeck and Elaine] live a good life, quite simple but we don't deny ourselves much. We see what theatre we want, and we eat well and sleep warm. I can't think of anything better."

by critics or by the general public as a particular type of writer who wrote only certain kinds of books. In 1957 Steinbeck published a short novel titled *The Short Reign of Pippin IV.*

Unlike most Steinbeck books, which had dramatic and serious subjects, *Pippin* is an amusing contemporary fantasy about the French monarchy. Although Steinbeck greatly enjoyed writing this book, his editor Pascal Covici disapproved. In a letter to Elizabeth Otis written in November 1956, Steinbeck expressed annoyance over what he felt was Covici's insistence that Steinbeck continue to turn out books similar in content to *The Grapes of Wrath:*

> Pat made me a little mad the other day. I am sure he doesn't like this kind of book but I'm pretty sure he was parroting Marshal [Best, another editor at Viking Press] about how many copies it would sell. . . . Pat treated me a little like Mickey Spillane [a popular mystery writer], and I know that he simply wants me to write *The Grapes of Wrath* over and over.[96]

Despite Covici's misgivings, however, *The Short Reign of Pippin IV* sold extremely well and became a selection of the Book-of-the-Month Club.

Quest of a Knight Errant

As Steinbeck's editor, Pascal Covici was primarily concerned that Steinbeck write commercially successful books. Steinbeck's principal objective, however, was to achieve artistic perfection. Steinbeck regarded the pursuit of excellence in writing as a spiritual journey, similar in many ways to the quest of a chivalrous knight for the Holy Grail. It was this belief that led him to begin, in 1956, a book based on a retelling of Sir Thomas Malory's novel *Morte d'Arthur*, which recounts the epic of King Arthur and the search of his knights for the Holy Grail.

Steinbeck had first read *Morte d'Arthur* as a child, and it was one of his favorite books. The French title notwithstanding, Malory's novel was written in medieval English, and although Steinbeck believed that the sound and structure of this language enhanced the book's spirit, he felt that modern readers would find the fifteenth century masterpiece too difficult to read. Inspired by Malory, Steinbeck decided to

An illustration from Morte d'Arthur, *one of Steinbeck's favorite books as a child. The book inspired Steinbeck to write a modern English version of the Arthurian legends.*

A Knightly Tribute

One of Steinbeck's fondest childhood memories was of leading a pony across a field of wild oats with his sister Mary riding bareback. Steinbeck chose to commemorate this memory of his sister in his written dedication to The Acts of King Arthur and His Noble Knights.

"When I was nine, I took siege with King Arthur's fellowship of knights most proud and worshipful as any alive.—In those days there was a great lack of hardy and noble-hearted squires to bear shield and sword, to buckle harness, and to succor wounded knights.—Then it chanced that squire-like duties fell to my sister of six years, who for gentle prowess had no peer living.—It sometimes happens in sadness and pity that faithful service is not appreciated, so my fair and loyal sister remained unrecognized as squire.—Wherefore this day I make amends within my power and raise her to knighthood and give her praise.—And from this hour she shall be called Sir Marie Steinbeck of Salinas Valley.—God give her worship without peril.

John Steinbeck of Monterey
Knight"

write his own version of the Arthurian legends. In a letter written to two friends, Mr. and Mrs. David Heyler Jr., on November 19, 1956, he explained what he hoped to accomplish:

> I am taking on something I have always wanted to do. That is the reduction of Thomas Malory's *Morte d'Arthur* to simple readable prose without adding or taking away anything, simply to put it into modern spelling and to translate the obsolete words to modern ones and to straighten out some of the more involved sentences.
>
> . . . It was the very first book I knew, and I have done considerable research over the years as my work will show. I loved the old forms, but most

people are put off by the spellings and obsolescences and the result is that all they have to go on is Prince Valiant and the movie versions.[97]

Steinbeck devoted three years of intense work to this book, which he titled *The Acts of King Arthur.* During the period of 1957-1959, Steinbeck and Elaine traveled to Europe three times to research the history of the Arthurian legends and to explore regions of England where the stories originated. Steinbeck also spent many long hours in libraries consulting the original published versions of *Morte d'Arthur.*

In *Morte d'Arthur,* Malory relates the saga of the quest by the Knights of the Round Table for the Holy Grail, a cup from which Christ was said to have drunk at the Last Supper. The Holy Grail is represented in Malory's book as a mystical symbol of ideal goodness. In *Morte d'Arthur*, the quest of Arthur's knights to attain the Holy Grail signified the individual's supreme aspiration to goodness. Steinbeck's endeavor to complete his book came to symbolize his own quest to achieve a personal ideal of honor and chivalry.

Translating and rewriting the Arthurian legends proved to be extremely difficult for Steinbeck. One of his great frustrations was the belief he eventually arrived at that he was unable to convey in modern language the emotions and chivalrous spirit of these tales. Steinbeck was to work intermittently on this volume for the rest of his life, but he would never complete the task to his satisfaction. His work was published posthumously, however, as *The Acts of King Arthur and His Noble Knights.*

In August 1959, Steinbeck wrote a letter to his friend Eugene Vinaver in which he confided his difficulties in writing this book, which was in many ways an expression of Steinbeck's own passion for literature combined with his love of gallantry:

I have a dreadful discontent with any efforts so far. They seem puny in the face of a hideous subject and I use the word in a Mallorian [sic] sense. How to capture the greatness? Who could improve on or change Launcelot's "For I take recorde of God, in you I have had myn earthly joye—" There it is. It can't be changed or moved.

. . . Good God, who could make that more moving? This is great poetry, passionate and epic and with also the stab of heartbreak. Can you see the problem? Do you know any answer?

This perplexity is like a great ache to me. You see a writer—like a knight—must aim at perfection, and failing, not fall back on the cushion [of pointing out] that there is no perfection. He must believe himself capable of perfection even when he fails. And that is probably why it is the loneliest profession in the world and the most lost. I come toward the ending of my life with the same ache for perfection I had as a child.[98]

Steinbeck would continue his quest for literary perfection until his death in 1968. His restless drive to write never diminished, and in the last nine years of his life Steinbeck continued to strive, achieving even greater excellence in his work despite declining health and advancing heart disease.

9 The Final Years

At the age of fifty-seven, John Steinbeck had led an active and adventurous life and had produced more than twenty books. Although his love of writing remained vital, the constant exertion of many years of strenuous work had taken its toll. On December 3, 1959, Steinbeck was stricken with a severe illness and hospitalized for two weeks. He had suffered two similar attacks while traveling in Europe in the 1950s. Although his physician gave no official diagnosis, Steinbeck's wife Elaine was convinced that her husband had suffered a series of strokes. While he convalesced in New York City that winter, Steinbeck pondered the direction his life and writing would take.

Steinbeck's illness reminded him that he was no longer a young man and that he had been writing books for a long time. In reviewing his life, Steinbeck felt a degree of discontent and restlessness regarding his work, on which he commented in a letter to Elizabeth Otis:

> I'm going to do what people call rest for a while. I don't quite know what that means—probably reorganize. I don't know what work is entailed, writing work, I mean, but I do know I have to slough off nearly fifteen years and go back and start again at the split path where I went wrong because it was easier.

After suffering a severe illness at the age of fifty-seven, Steinbeck was forced to take time out of his busy schedule to relax. Here, he bird-watches at his Sag Harbor home.

A Ceaseless Quest

Throughout his life, Steinbeck remained steadfast in the conviction that writing was a solitary quest to achieve perfection. He had first been exposed to this philosophy by his Stanford professor, Edith Mirrielees. In June 1961, the world-famous author wrote a letter to his friend John Murphy, restating this belief.

"Nine tenths of a writer's life do not admit of any companion nor friend nor associate. And until one makes peace with loneliness and accepts it as a part of the profession, as celibacy is a part of priesthood, until then there are times of dreadful dread. I am just as terrified of my next book as I was of my first. It doesn't get easier. It gets harder and more heartbreaking and finally, it must be that one must accept the failure which is the end of every writer's life no matter what stir he may have made. In himself he must fail as Launcelot failed—for the Grail is not a cup. It's a promise that skips ahead—it's a carrot on a stick and it never fails to draw us on. So it is that I would greatly prefer to die in the middle of a sentence in the middle of a book and so leave it as all life must be—unfinished. That's the law, the great law. Principles of notoriety or publicity or even public acceptance do not apply. Greatness is not shared by a man who is great. And by the same token—if he should want it—he can't possibly get near it."

True things gradually disappeared and shiny easy things took their place. . . . I tell you this because if I am able to go back, the first efforts will be as painful as those of a child learning to balance one block on top of another. I'll have to learn all over again about true things. I don't have any other choice.[99]

As Steinbeck began to feel better he became increasingly uncomfortable with the concern his family and friends were expressing over his health. Steinbeck had always prided himself on being self-reliant. He worried that people's well-meaning insistence that he curtail his activities might diminish his independence. Steinbeck was aware of the seriousness of his illness but resolved to continue his work and to live the remaining years of his life as fully as possible. "I will not take it easy," he wrote to Elizabeth Otis after returning from the hospital. "But I will throw everything I possess against whatever world I can move in the effort to take it right."[100]

Part of Steinbeck's depression regarding his writing at this time was due to his inability to complete his book on the Arthurian legends. Frustrated, he began considering other literary projects that would provide new creative challenges.

A Critical View of the "American Dream"

Steinbeck was also concerned about his ability to raise his two sons, Thom and John, in a society that in his estimation had become corrupt and immoral. "It is very hard to raise boys to love and respect virtue and learning," Steinbeck wrote to secretary to the United Nations, Dag Hammarskjold, "when the tools of success are chicanery, treachery, self-interest, laziness and cynicism or when charity is deductible, the courts venal, the highest political official placid, vain, slothful and illiterate."[101]

What Steinbeck viewed as the moral erosion of American character, as a result of greed and selfishness, became the

Steinbeck became concerned about his ability to raise his two sons John, left, and Thom, in a society that he believed had become corrupt and immoral.

theme of his final novel, *The Winter of Our Discontent*. Steinbeck began writing this book in the spring of 1960. By mid-July he had completed the first draft, and the book was published in 1961.

The Winter of Our Discontent focuses on the moral dilemma of its main character, Ethan Hawley. Although a proud descendant of New England aristocracy, Hawley works as a clerk in the grocery store of a seaport town once owned by his family. By instinct a man of principle, Hawley is dismayed to perceive in himself betrayal and compromise of his personal code of ethics as he obsessively pursues the "American dream," as represented by material wealth.

A Journey in Search of America

Shortly after completing *The Winter of Our Discontent*, Steinbeck decided to embark on a solo trip across the United States, visiting various sites along the way. Steinbeck intended to make this journey in a customized camper, which he planned to have mounted on a three-quarter ton pickup truck. He had decided to christen the truck *Rocinante*, after the mare Don Quixote rode in his adventures. It was to be a great adventure and a long pilgrimage, which Steinbeck would make with only a tall blue poodle named Charley for company.

Steinbeck's wife and friends watched him prepare for this adventure with misgivings. They advised him not to go, believing that so long a journey could be hazardous for a man alone, particularly for someone fifty-eight years old. Despite their objections however, Steinbeck remained determined to make the journey,

A Personal Odyssey

As Steinbeck prepared to embark on his cross-country journey, many people were comparing him to Don Quixote. This passage from a letter to Pascal Covici, in Steinbeck: A Life in Letters, *reveals Steinbeck's determination to proceed with his trip.*

"My truck is ordered for the trip I spoke of about the country. It will come in the middle of August. I plan to leave after Labor Day. I know you approve of the trip and know how necessary it is to me but there are others who find it so Quixotic that I am calling it Operation Windmills and have named my truck *Rocinante*. But regardless of advice, I shall go. Sure I want to go and am excited about it, but more than that—I have to go. And only I can judge that necessity. I know you understand this. I don't know what I shall find nor feel about what I shall find. For that reason I am making no literary plans in advance to warp what I see. As again in the *Sea of Cortez*—a trip is a thing in itself and must be kept so."

and on the morning of September 23, 1960, he and his companion Charley boarded *Rocinante* and left New York.

Travels with Charley: In Search of America, the volume describing this pilgrimage, was published in 1962. In the opening chapter, Steinbeck candidly relates the motives that compelled him to make the journey:

For many years I have traveled in many parts of the world. In America I live in New York, or dip into Chicago or San Francisco. But New York is no more America than Paris is France or London is England. Thus I discovered that I did not know my own country. I, an American writer, writing about America, was working from memory, and the memory is at best a faulty, warpy reservoir. I had not heard the speech of America, smelled the grass and trees and sewage, seen its hills and water, its color and quality of light. I knew the change only from books and newspapers. But more than this, I had not felt the country for twenty-five years. In short, I was writing of something I did not know about, and it seems to me that in a so-called writer this is criminal. My memories were distorted by twenty-five intervening years.[102]

Steinbeck's cross-country journey, which lasted for eleven weeks, climaxed in a return to Salinas, California, the author's birthplace. Before departing from California to return to his home in New York, Steinbeck drove to the crest of Fremont's Peak and, with Charley, climbed to the same mountain summit that he had explored as a boy.

Here on these high rocks my memory myth repaired itself. "You wouldn't

The Nobel Prize

Travels with Charley relates the story of Steinbeck's eleven-week journey across the United States.

know, my Charley, that right down there, in that little valley, I fished for trout with your namesake, my Uncle Charley. And over there—see where I am pointing—my mother shot a wildcat. Can you see that darker place over there? Well, that's a tiny canyon with a clear and lovely stream bordered with wild azaleas and ringed with big oaks. And on one of those oaks my father burned his name with a hot iron together with the name of the girl he loved."

I printed it once more on my eyes, south, west, and north, and then we hurried away from the permanent and changeless past where my mother is always shooting a wildcat and my father is always burning his name with his love.[103]

On the morning of October 25, 1962, a few months after the publication of *Travels with Charley*, Steinbeck switched on the television set in his Sag Harbor home to hear the announcement, "John Steinbeck has been awarded the Nobel Prize for literature." The news came as a complete surprise to the Steinbecks. Elaine was so excited that in her distraction, she placed a pan of frying bacon in the refrigerator. Steinbeck, however, immediately cabled Anders Osterling, the secretary of the Swedish Academy, that he would happily attend the award ceremony in Stockholm.

Later at a press conference, Steinbeck humorously remarked that the prospect of receiving the prestigious award left him feeling "wrapped and shellacked." When asked to explain, he replied: "Ever see a fishbowl that's going to crack? You wrap it and shellack it. I don't feel very real."[104]

Tradition required that each winner of a Nobel Prize deliver an acceptance speech before the Swedish Academy. Steinbeck realized that the occasion would offer him an important opportunity to address the world with a personal statement about his humanitarian beliefs. The address Steinbeck delivered from the podium at Stockholm was direct, eloquent, and brief. Within its content, he expressed his personal convictions about literature.

Literature was not promulgated by a pale and emasculated critical priesthood singing their litanies in empty churches—nor is it a game for the cloistered elect, the tinhorn mendicants of low calorie despair.

Steinbeck accepts the Nobel Prize for literature in 1962.

Literature is as old as speech. It grew out of human need for it, and has not changed except to become more needed.[105]

After his return from Stockholm, Steinbeck continued to ponder possible new literary projects. The journey across the United States that had led to *Travels with Charley* had increased Steinbeck's realization of the great complexity of the American nation. He was particularly angered by the intense racial bigotry and hatred that existed in the country. In *Travels with Charley*, Steinbeck graphically described a scene in New Orleans, where discrimination against black schoolchildren had ended in violence.

A Character Study of Americans

The moral decay of America continued to trouble Steinbeck, although he had written about it in *The Winter of Our Discontent*. He shared some of these thoughts in a letter written to Pascal Covici from Sag Harbor:

> In all my travels I saw very little poverty, I mean the grinding terrifying poorness of the Thirties. That at least was real and tangible. No, it was a kind of sickness, a kind of wasting disease. There were wishes but no wants. And underneath it all the building energy like gasses in a corpse. When that explodes I tremble to think what will be the result. Over and over I thought we lack the pressures that make men strong and the anguish that makes men great. The pressures are debts, the desires are for more material toys and the anguish is boredom. Through time, the nation has become a discontented land.[106]

In February 1965, Steinbeck began work on a book of photographs and essays about what he felt to be the positive and negative elements of our national character. "I may have to run for my life when it comes out," Steinbeck wrote to actor John Huston. "I am taking 'the American' apart like a watch to see what makes him tick and some very curious things are emerging."[107]

The volume was published in 1966 under the title *America and Americans*; it would be Steinbeck's final book. The text presents a character study of Americans and a personal and interpretive review of their evolution from emigrants in a melting pot into a national people: "America did not exist." Steinbeck wrote in the book's opening chapter:

> Four centuries of work, of bloodshed, of loneliness and fear created this land. We built America and the process made us Americans—a new breed, rooted in all races, stained and tinted with all colors, a seeming ethnic anarchy. Then in a little, little time, we became more alike than we were different—a new society; not great, but fitted by our very faults for greatness, *E Pluribus Unum*.[108]

Vietnam Correspondent

During the last years of his life, Steinbeck became deeply involved in studying the political and military situations of the

---

"I Am Not a Liar"

In a letter to Mr. and Mrs. Robert Wallsten excerpted from Steinbeck: A Life in Letters, *Steinbeck relates his publisher's concern over the eyewitness account of an incident of racial violence in* Travels with Charley. *Despite ill health and his publisher's fears, Steinbeck was determined to uphold the integrity of his writing.*

"The last section of *Travels with Charley* has been giving the publishers trouble. It deals with some rough things in the south. . . . But Viking [the publisher] wants to keep it tough and still not be sued. And I have been so bloody weak that I just don't give a damn.

It seems to me that everybody in America is scared of everything mostly before it happens. I finally sent word that what reputation I had was not based on timidity or on playing safe. And I hope that is over. What I wrote either happened or I am a liar and I am not a liar. And I know that truth is no defense against libel. But there is no way of being safe except by being completely unsafe. And in the succeeding months I don't think that being careful of my health is likely to improve it. Rather it will give me another sickness, and I hate it. The whole world is torn up, if the papers tell the truth and the papers themselves may be the paper tiger we hear so much about. Everywhere are paper tigers."

While on assignment in Vietnam for Newsday, *Steinbeck accompanied American troops on dangerous patrols and helicopter missions.*

Vietnam War. In spite of declining health, he accepted an assignment as a correspondent for *Newsday* magazine to cover the war. Accompanied by his wife Elaine, who worked as his assistant, Steinbeck departed for Vietnam in November 1966. While Elaine remained in hotels to file her husband's reports, Steinbeck accompanied American troops on numerous patrols and helicopter missions.

Although he doubted the political wisdom of American involvement in Vietnam, Steinbeck came to admire the American soldiers who fought in the war. The series of articles he dispatched to *Newsday* were written primarily to convey the individual soldier's perspective of the war. The perilous extent of Steinbeck's involvement with American combat patrols is very apparent in this excerpt from a report filed with *Newsday:*

> Out of the undergrowth, thicker than any I have ever seen, faces, or really only eyes, appear. Mottled helmets

and fatigues disappear against the background. Faces black or white from sweat and dirt have become a kind of universal reddish gray. Only the eyes are alive and lively. And when we settle and the rotor stops, the mouths open and they are men, and what men. Can you understand the quick glow of pride one feels in just belonging to the same species of these men?

> D troop. . . smelled of sweat, hardworking sweat. On the back of every helmet, under the strap, was a plastic spray bottle of insect repellent. I went into a V.C. [Viet Cong] trail so deep and covered with jungle that you are in perpetual steaming dusk. It was one of the transport trails over which they force the local people to carry their supplies. . . .

> I started down the dark cave of a trail and a sergeant quite a bit bigger than a breadbox called "Don't go far. It's booby trapped.". . . I didn't go far.[109]

A Native Son Returns Home

The Steinbecks returned to New York in the third week of April 1967. Shortly after their arrival in Sag Harbor, Steinbeck collapsed in pain from a back injury he had suffered while touring Southeast Asia. Because of his age and a diagnosis of advancing heart disease, physicians decided against surgery. Steinbeck's back condition was instead treated with medication, and he spent the summer in Sag Harbor in considerable pain.

Despite his illness, Steinbeck continued to make hopeful plans to write, and he said wistfully in a letter to Elizabeth Otis that he wished

to go out to my little house on the point, sharpen fifty pencils and put out a yellow pad. Early in the morning to hear what the birds are saying and to pass the time of day with Angel [Steinbeck's dog] and then to hunch up my chair to my writing board and to set down with words—"Once upon a time, . . ."[110]

In July 1968, Steinbeck experienced difficulty in breathing and was brought by ambulance to a hospital in New York City, where he suffered a severe heart attack. A

An Alarming Corruption

Steinbeck's disenchantment over what he perceived to be America's moral decay in the 1960s led him to write his last novel, The Winter of Our Discontent. *In it, Steinbeck described the corruption of a fictitious New England community, which he believed to be typical of the depravity that he saw affecting the entire nation.*

"Now a slow, deliberate encirclement was moving on New Baytown, and it was set in motion by honorable men. If it succeeded, they would be thought not crooked but clever. And if a factor they had overlooked moved in, would that be immoral or dishonorable? I think that would depend on whether or not it was successful. To most of the world success is never bad. I remember how, when Hitler moved unchecked and triumphant, many honorable men sought and found virtues in him. And Mussolini made the trains run on time, and Vichy collaborated for the good of France, and whatever else Stalin was, he was strong. Strength and success—they are above morality, above criticism. It seems, then, that it is not what you do, but how you do it and what you call it. Is there a check in men, deep in them, that stops or punishes? There doesn't seem to be. The only punishment is for failure. In effect no crime is committed unless a criminal is caught."

month later, despite strong objections from the medical staff, he returned to Sag Harbor to recuperate. As his health continued to fail and death appeared imminent, Steinbeck's wife Elaine was constantly at his bedside. Shortly before his death, Steinbeck remarked that "No man should be buried in alien soil." Elaine replied, "I know what you are telling me. You won't be."[111]

On the morning of December 20, 1968, John Steinbeck lapsed into a coma and shortly afterward died peacefully in his sleep. A brief funeral service was held at St. James Episcopal Church on Madison Avenue in New York City. Faithful to her promise, Elaine Steinbeck and Steinbeck's son Thom returned the writer's ashes to California, where they were interred in the Hamilton family plot in the Garden of Memories at Salinas.

Perhaps one of the most fitting tributes to John Steinbeck's life and work may be found in a letter from Steinbeck's editor Pascal Covici, written in 1958:

> That you were born and in some small way I have been of use to you in bringing your books to light means a great deal to me, possibly infinitely more than you may ever realize.
>
> When I look back at the long list of your books, I am truly astounded. And if you don't write another book,

The author at his home in Sag Harbor, where he died in 1968. He is pictured here with his poodle Charley, who accompanied him on his cross-country journey.

you have written your name in American literature for as long as the human race can read. For you too, have the poetry, the compassion, the laughter and tears we find in Cervantes, and Dickens and Mark Twain. A reading of your work will always add something new to one's imagination and will always have something to say.[112]

Notes

Introduction: Making People Understand Each Other

1. John Steinbeck, *Steinbeck: A Life in Letters.* Edited by Elaine Steinbeck and Robert Wallsten. New York: Viking Press, 1975.
2. Jackson J. Benson, *The True Adventures of John Steinbeck, Writer.* New York: Viking Press, 1984.
3. Steinbeck, *A Life in Letters.*
4. John Steinbeck, Nobel Prize acceptance speech, in *Vogue* magazine, March 1, 1963.

Chapter 1: Early Struggles

5. John Steinbeck, *East of Eden.* New York: Viking Press, 1952.
6. Steinbeck, *East of Eden.*
7. Benson, *The True Adventures of John Steinbeck, Writer.*
8. Benson, *The True Adventures of John Steinbeck, Writer.*
9. John Steinbeck, *The Acts of King Arthur and His Noble Knights.* Toronto, Canada: McGraw-Hill Ryerson Ltd., 1976.
10. Benson, *The True Adventures of John Steinbeck, Writer.*
11. Benson, *The True Adventures of John Steinbeck, Writer.*
12. Benson, *The True Adventures of John Steinbeck, Writer.*
13. Benson, *The True Adventures of John Steinbeck, Writer.*
14. Benson, *The True Adventures of John Steinbeck, Writer.*
15. Steinbeck, *A Life in Letters.*
16. Steinbeck, *A Life in Letters.*

Chapter 2: California Camelot

17. Steinbeck, *A Life in Letters.*
18. Steinbeck, *A Life in Letters.*
19. Steinbeck, *A Life in Letters.*
20. Steinbeck, *A Life in Letters.*
21. Steinbeck, *A Life in Letters.*
22. John Steinbeck, "A Primer on the 30s," *Esquire,* June 1960.
23. Steinbeck, *A Life in Letters.*
24. Steinbeck, *A Life in Letters.*
25. Steinbeck, *A Life in Letters.*
26. John Steinbeck, *Tortilla Flat.* New York: Covici-Friede, 1935; New York: Viking Press, 1953.
27. Steinbeck, *A Life in Letters.*
28. Steinbeck, *A Life in Letters.*

Chapter 3: Poverty and Persistence

29. Benson, *The True Adventures of John Steinbeck, Writer.*
30. Steinbeck, *A Life in Letters.*
31. Steinbeck, *A Life in Letters.*
32. John Milton, quoted in Steinbeck, *A Life in Letters.*
33. Steinbeck, *A Life in Letters.*
34. Benson, *The True Adventures of John Steinbeck, Writer.*
35. Benson, *The True Adventures of John Steinbeck, Writer.*
36. Steinbeck, *A Life in Letters.*
37. Steinbeck, *A Life in Letters.*
38. John Steinbeck, *Of Mice and Men.* New York: Covici-Friede, 1937; New York: Viking Press, 1953.
39. Steinbeck, *Of Mice and Men.*
40. Steinbeck, *Of Mice and Men.*
41. Steinbeck, *A Life in Letters.*

Chapter 4: An Exalted Endeavor

42. Benson, *The True Adventures of John Steinbeck, Writer.*

43. Steinbeck, *A Life in Letters.*

44. Steinbeck, *A Life in Letters.*

45. Benson, *The True Adventures of John Steinbeck, Writer.*

46. Steinbeck, *A Life in Letters.*

47. Benson, *The True Adventures of John Steinbeck, Writer.*

48. Steinbeck, *A Life in Letters.*

49. Benson, *The True Adventures of John Steinbeck, Writer.*

50. John Steinbeck, *The Grapes of Wrath.* New York: Viking Press, 1939.

51. Steinbeck, *The Grapes of Wrath.*

52. Steinbeck, *The Grapes of Wrath.*

53. Steinbeck, *The Grapes of Wrath.*

54. Benson, *The True Adventures of John Steinbeck, Writer.*

55. John Steinbeck, *Working Days, The Journals of "The Grapes of Wrath."* New York: Penguin Books, 1990.

56. Steinbeck, *A Life in Letters.*

Chapter 5: Eventful Years

57. Steinbeck, *A Life in Letters.*

58. Steinbeck, *A Life in Letters.*

59. Steinbeck, *A Life in Letters.*

60. Steinbeck, *A Life in Letters.*

61. Benson, *The True Adventures of John Steinbeck, Writer.*

62. Steinbeck, *Working Days.*

63. Steinbeck, *A Life in Letters.*

64. Benson, *The True Adventures of John Steinbeck, Writer.*

65. John Steinbeck, *Once There Was a War.* New York: Viking Press, 1948, 1958.

Chapter 6: Return to California

66. Benson, *The True Adventures of John Steinbeck, Writer.*

67. Benson, *The True Adventures of John Steinbeck, Writer.*

68. Steinbeck, *A Life in Letters.*

69. Steinbeck, *A Life in Letters.*

70. John Steinbeck, *Cannery Row.* New York: Viking Press, 1945, 1953.

71. Benson, *The True Adventures of John Steinbeck, Writer.*

72. Benson, *The True Adventures of John Steinbeck, Writer.*

73. Benson, *The True Adventures of John Steinbeck, Writer.*

74. Steinbeck, *A Life in Letters.*

75. Steinbeck, *A Life in Letters.*

76. Steinbeck, *A Life in Letters.*

77. Benson, *The True Adventures of John Steinbeck, Writer.*

78. Steinbeck, *A Life in Letters.*

79. Steinbeck, *A Life in Letters.*

80. Steinbeck, *A Life in Letters.*

Chapter 7: Turbulent Years

81. Steinbeck, *A Life in Letters.*

82. Benson, *The True Adventures of John Steinbeck, Writer.*

83. Benson, *The True Adventures of John Steinbeck, Writer.*

84. Steinbeck, *A Life in Letters.*

85. Benson, *The True Adventures of John Steinbeck, Writer.*

86. Steinbeck, *A Life in Letters.*

87. Benson, *The True Adventures of John Steinbeck, Writer.*

88. John Steinbeck, *Journal of a Novel: The "East of Eden" Letters.* New York: Viking Press, 1969.

89. Steinbeck, *Journal of a Novel.*

90. Steinbeck, *Journal of a Novel.*

Chapter 8: In Search of New Challenges

91. Steinbeck, *A Life in Letters.*

92. Steinbeck, *A Life in Letters.*

93. Benson, *The True Adventures of John Steinbeck, Writer.*

94. Steinbeck, *A Life in Letters.*

95. Benson, *The True Adventures of John Steinbeck, Writer.*

96. Benson, *The True Adventures of John Steinbeck, Writer.*

97. Steinbeck, *A Life in Letters.*

98. Steinbeck, *A Life in Letters.*

Chapter 9: The Final Years

99. Steinbeck, *A Life in Letters.*

100. Steinbeck, *A Life in Letters.*

101. Steinbeck, *A Life in Letters.*

102. John Steinbeck, *Travels with Charley: In Search of America*, New York: Viking Press, 1962.

103. Steinbeck, *Travels with Charley.*

104. Benson, *The True Adventures of John Steinbeck, Writer.*

105. Steinbeck, Nobel Prize acceptance speech.

106. Steinbeck, *A Life in Letters.*

107. Steinbeck, *A Life in Letters.*

108. John Steinbeck, *America and Americans.* New York: Viking Press, 1966.

109. Benson, *The True Adventures of John Steinbeck, Writer.*

110. Benson, *The True Adventures of John Steinbeck, Writer.*

111. Benson, *The True Adventures of John Steinbeck, Writer.*

112. Benson, *The True Adventures of John Steinbeck, Writer.*

For Further Reading

Richard Astro, *John Steinbeck and Edward F. Ricketts*. Minneapolis: University of Minnesota Press, 1973. Scholarly account of Steinbeck's friendship with marine biologist Edward Ricketts, offering an analysis of Ricketts's intellectual and philosophical influence on Steinbeck's writing.

Jackson J. Benson, *The True Adventures of John Steinbeck, Writer*. New York: Viking Press, 1984. Meticulously researched and comprehensively written biography of John Steinbeck, which offers a thoughtful and sympathetic perspective of Steinbeck as man and writer.

Peter Lisca, *The Wide World of John Steinbeck*. New Brunswick, NJ: Rutgers University Press, 1958. A single-volume collection of literary critiques of Steinbeck's books spanning his first published work, *Cup of Gold* (1929) to *The Short Reign of Pippin IV* (1957). It is a valuable source of reference material regarding the author but somewhat dry and fragmented in its composition.

Edward F. Ricketts and Jack Calvin, *Between Pacific Tides*. Palo Alto, CA: Stanford University Press, 1939. Scholarly ecological sea study by Steinbeck's close friend Ed Ricketts and an associate. The book, which appeared in print in the same year as Steinbeck's *Grapes of Wrath*, offers an interesting opportunity to contrast the respective literary styles of Steinbeck and Ricketts.

Brian St. Pierre, *John Steinbeck: The California Years*. San Francisco: Chronicle Books, 1983. Affectionately written study of Steinbeck's life with a strong focus on the subject's California origin. The book primarily chronicles Steinbeck's life as a writer from his childhood to the writing of *East of Eden* and includes a brief account of his later years and death.

John Steinbeck, *Cup of Gold: A Life of Sir Henry Morgan, Buccaneer, with Occasional Reference to History*. New York: Robert McBride, 1929. Steinbeck's first published novel, written when he was twenty-six years old, is about the famed privateer, Sir Henry Morgan. It is particularly interesting as Steinbeck's first literary effort and reveals the strong romantic and mystical strains in his writing at that time of his life.

John Steinbeck, *Steinbeck: A Life in Letters*. Edited by Elaine A. Steinbeck and Robert Wallsten. New York: Viking Press, 1975. Impressive volume of selected journal entries and personal correspondence by John Steinbeck.

John Steinbeck, *Tortilla Flat*. New York: Covici-Friede, 1935; New York: Viking Press, 1953. Steinbeck's first commercially successful novel. The book was Steinbeck's first attempt at composing a modern version of the Arthurian saga. Written with humor and pathos, *Tortilla Flat* is descriptively rich with the local color of Monterey as Steinbeck knew it in the 1930s and projects the author's love for the Spanish and Italian that flourished in the region at the time.

John Steinbeck, *The Winter of Our Discontent*. New York: Viking Press, 1961; New York, Bantam Books, 1962. Steinbeck's last novel reflects the author's disillusionment over what he believed to be the moral decay of America. Its confident and ironic, philosophical literary style was strongly characteristic of Steinbeck's later work.

John Steinbeck IV, *In Touch*. New York: Alfred A. Knopf, 1976. Steinbeck's younger son wrote this memoir recalling the controversy arising over his alleged involvement with marijuana while serving in the army during the Vietnam War. The book contains some brief and rather formal references to the author's relationship with his father.

Steinbeck, The Man and His Work. Edited by Richard Astro and Tesumaro Hayashi. Corvallis: Oregon State Press, 1972. A scholarly reference work assessing Steinbeck's literary career in a book-length collection of essays by several scholars.

Additional Works Consulted

John Steinbeck, *The Acts of King Arthur and His Noble Knights*. Toronto, Canada: McGraw-Hill Ryerson Ltd., 1976. Published posthumously. Steinbeck spent several years researching the work. The book is particularly significant because it represents Steinbeck's dedicated endeavor to capture the essence of the Arthurian saga in modern language.

John Steinbeck, *America and Americans*. New York: Viking Press, 1966. A series of essays written as character studies of the American people and published with numerous photographs. Much of the material is a progression of Steinbeck's impressions about America and its people first written about in *Travels with Charley*.

John Steinbeck, *Burning Bright*. New York: Viking Press, 1950. Generally considered to be one of Steinbeck's minor works, this book was an attempt by him to combine a novella and theatrical screenplay into a single work.

John Steinbeck, *Cannery Row*. New York: Viking Press, 1953. Steinbeck's short novel set in the Monterey waterfront community of Cannery Row is rich in character studies drawn from Steinbeck's memories and impressions of people he had known in the region. Particularly significant is the introduction of the character of Doc, inspired by Steinbeck's friend, Ed Ricketts. The book is actually an allegorical presentation of Steinbeck's ecological theories. He compares the interaction of the residents of Cannery Row to the natural community of a Pacific tide pool.

John Steinbeck, *In Dubious Battle*. New York: Covici-Friede, 1936. Considered by many to be the forerunner of *The Grapes of Wrath*, the novel relates a grim and taut story about the suppressive tyranny inflicted upon migrant farmworkers during a violent California fruit strike.

John Steinbeck, *The Forgotten Village*. New York: Viking Press, 1941. Published in book form and illustrated with photographs, *The Forgotten Village* is actually a short story evolved from an original handwritten manuscript of thirty-six pages. The tale relates, in documentary form, the dilemma shared by the inhabitants of a primitive Mexican village when they are confronted with the challenge of either adapting to the methods of modern science or perishing from illness through the ignorance of superstition.

John Steinbeck, *The Grapes of Wrath*. New York: Viking Press, 1939. This book continues to remain Steinbeck's most famous work and the novel by which he is best known. Relates the stirring account of a migrant family's courageous trek to California in search of their promised land. The novel won the Pulitzer Prize in 1940.

John Steinbeck, *Of Mice and Men*. New York: Viking Press, 1953. Steinbeck's memorable novella about two men and their ill-fated struggle to attain home and happiness in the harsh and impoverished environment of the California farmlands during the Great Depression.

John Steinbeck, *The Moon Is Down*. New York: Viking Press, 1942. Somber and suspenseful novel regarding the events of a fictitious European village occupied by Nazi invaders during World War II. Originally written by Steinbeck as an assignment from the federal government to aid the American war effort.

John Steinbeck, *Once There Was a War*. New York: Viking Press, 1958. Edited volume of selected compilation of dispatches originally written by Steinbeck in World War II, reprinted in book form. It provides a provocative retrospective view of Steinbeck's frontline combat experiences.

John Steinbeck, *The Pearl*. New York: Viking Press, 1947. One of Steinbeck's most popular short novels. Inspired from a folk tale Steinbeck had heard during his travels in Mexico, *The Pearl* is a memorable tragic allegory of good and evil written in haunting and lyrical form.

John Steinbeck, *Travels with Charley: In Search of America*. New York: Viking Press, 1962. Steinbeck's leisurely account of his cross-country journey over the United States with a poodle named Charley provides a rare insight into the author's personality. The journey was of special importance to Steinbeck as a personal attempt to rediscover the land of his birth.

John Steinbeck, *The Wayward Bus*. New York: Viking Press, 1947. Humorous novel about the travels of a busload of passengers embarked upon a series of vagabond adventures. The book was written by Steinbeck as an allegory employing a dilapidated bus as a microcosmic symbol of a human community.

John Steinbeck, *The Winter of Our Discontent*. New York: Penguin Books, 1962. Steinbeck's last novel, about the moral dilemma of a disenchanted New England businessman, reflects the author's own concern over what he perceived to be the moral decay of America.

John Steinbeck, *Working Days*. New York: Penguin Books, 1990. Edited compilation of ninety-nine journal entries written by Steinbeck during the summer and fall of 1938, chronicling many of the author's personal thoughts and work habits during the writing of *The Grapes of Wrath*. *Working Days* is similar to *Journal of a Novel* in the respect that both books provide interesting insights to Steinbeck's creative ethics and philosophy as a writer.

Index

The Acts of King Arthur and His Noble Knights (Steinbeck), 13, 90-91
Albee, George, 25, 28, 36, 37, 38, 80
America and Americans (Steinbeck), 98
Arthurian theme
    Steinbeck's use of, 30-33, 89-91

Ballou, Robert, 25-26, 27, 29-31
Benét, Stephen Vincent, 58
Benson, Jackson J., 12, 15, 17, 23, 28
Berry, Tom, 56
Beskow, Bo, 71, 74, 75, 77
Best, Marshall, 89
Bombs Away (Steinbeck), 59
Book-of-the-Month Club, 6
Brando, Marlon, 79
Buck, Jules, 78-79, 86-87
Buck, Pearl, 52
Burning Bright (Steinbeck), 77, 87

Cabell, James Branch, 21
Cannery Row (Steinbeck), 65-67
    plot outline, 65-66
Capa, Robert, 72
Cape, Jonathan, 26, 27
Cape and Smith (publishers), 25, 26
Cathcart, Robert, 15, 17
Cervantes, Miguel de, 101
Chaney, Lon, Jr., 41, 56
Circle Award, 42
Clark, Mark, 61
Collier's magazine, 84
Collins, Tom, 44-45
Commonwealth Club, 33, 44
communism
    Steinbeck's lack of alliance with, 36
Conger, Gwyndolyn. *See* Steinbeck, Gwyndolyn Conger

(second wife of Steinbeck)
Covici, Pascal, 32-33, 37-39, 44, 48-49, 57, 89
    as supportive friend of Steinbeck, 76-77, 83
    letters from Steinbeck, 51, 55, 61, 65, 70, 73, 80, 95, 97
    letters to Steinbeck, 72, 101
    tribute to Steinbeck, 101
Covici-Friede (publishers), 33, 48
Cup of Gold (Steinbeck), 16, 19-21, 23

Darwell, Jane, 50
Day, Grove A., 20-21
Dickens, Charles, 101
Dissonant Symphony (Steinbeck), 22-23
Dust Bowl, 43, 54

East of Eden (Steinbeck), 7, 10, 80-84
ecological philosophy of Steinbeck, 66
Esquire magazine, 29

Farm Security Administration, 45
Faulkner, William, 84
Field, Betty, 56
FIS (U.S. Foreign Information Service), 58
Fonda, Henry, 49
The Forgotten Village (Steinbeck), 57-58
Fortune magazine, 46

Gabilan, El (yearbook), 13
Garfield, John, 38
Gold Medal (Commonwealth Club), 33
The Grapes of Wrath (Steinbeck), 7, 8, 9, 48-55
    banned in some regions, 52
    movie version of, 49-50, 56

    plot outline of, 49-52
    Pulitzer Prize for, 58
Great Depression, 8, 29 , 39
Gregory, Sue, 30-31
Guinzburg, Harold, 57

Hadden, Ann, 39
Hammarskjold, Dag, 94
Hammerstein, Oscar, II, 87-88
"The Harvest Grapes" (Steinbeck), 45
Hemingway, Ernest, 84, 86
Heyler, Mr. and Mrs. David, Jr., 90
Holt, Guy, 17-18
Horton, Chase, 86
Huston, John, 98

"I Go Back to Ireland" (Steinbeck), 85
In Dubious Battle (Steinbeck), 8, 35-38

Jackson, Henry, 42
John Day & Company, 18
Jonathan Cape & Robert Ballou, Inc., 26, 27
Journal of a Novel: The "East of Eden" Letters (Steinbeck), 82-83

Kaufman, George S., 42
Kazan, Elia, 78, 87-88
Lamarr, Hedy, 38
Lange, Dorothea, 43
Life magazine, 45-46, 69
The Log from the "The Sea of Cortez" (Steinbeck), 57, 66, 95
London, Jack, 14-15
Los Angeles Times, 33
Lovejoy, Ritchie, 66, 69-70, 74
Lovejoy, Tal, 74
Lyman, Mildred, 77

McBride & Company, 17-18, 20
McIntosh, Mavis, 24-25, 27, 31

McIntosh & Otis, 25, 27, 32, 42, 48, 77

Malory, Sir Thomas, 13, 32, 89-90

marine biology
Steinbeck's interest and research in, 55-57

Meredith, Burgess, 41, 56

Miller, Amasa "Ted," 17-18, 20, 23, 28, 34

Milton, John, 36

Mirrielees, Edith Ronald, 15, 93

Monterey Trader, 46-47

The Moon Is Down (Steinbeck), 58-59

moral erosion of Americans
Steinbeck on, 94, 97-98, 100

Morgan, Henry, 19-20

Morte d'Arthur (Malory), 13, 32, 89-90

"The Murderer" (Steinbeck), 6

Murphy, John, 93

Needham, Wilbur, 33

Newsday, 99

New York American, 16-18

New York Drama Critics' Circle Award, 42

New York Herald Tribune, 61-62

New York Tribune, 72

Nobel Prize, 7, 96-97
Steinbeck's acceptance speech, 9, 96-97

nonteleology, 41-42

North American Review, 28-29

Of Mice and Men (Steinbeck), 7, 8, 39-44
Book-of-the-Month Club selection, 6
movie version, 41, 56
plot outline, 40-41
stage version, 42
symbolic content, 40

O. Henry prize, 6

Okies, 8, 9, 43, 47

Once There Was a War (Steinbeck), 62-63

Otis, Elizabeth, 24-25, 27
letters from Steinbeck, 35, 37, 44-45, 47-49, 56, 67, 69, 86-89, 92-93

Pacific Laboratories, Inc., 24

paisanos, 30-31

Pan American Films, 70-71

Paradise Lost (Milton), 36

Paramount Studios, 38

The Pastures of Heaven (Steinbeck), 25-26

The Pearl (Steinbeck), 67-68, 71
movie version, 68, 71

Phelan Award, 39

Pilgrim's Progress (Bunyon), 13

Pipe Dream (Steinbeck), 87-88

"The Red Pony" (Steinbeck), 28-29

The Red Pony (Steinbeck), 29

Ricketts, Edward, 27, 39
injury and death of, 73-74
meeting and long friendship with Steinbeck, 23-24, 29-30, 65, 69-70
Mexican research with Steinbeck, 55-57

Robert McBride & Company, 17-18, 20

Rodgers, Richard, 87-88

Roosevelt, Eleanor, 52, 54

Roosevelt, Franklin D., 52

Salinas High School, 13-14

Sandburg, Carl, 58

San Francisco News, 43, 45

Saroyan, William, 58

Scott, Zachary, 79

The Sea of Cortez (Steinbeck), 57, 66, 95

Sheffield, Carlton, 19, 32, 65, 85, 88

The Short Reign of Pippin IV (Steinbeck), 89

Something That Happened. See Of Mice and Men

Southern Pacific Milling Company, 11

Spreckles Sugar Company, 11

Stanford University, 14-16

"Starvation Under the Orange Trees" (Steinbeck), 47

Steinbeck, Carol Henning (first wife of Steinbeck), 22, 30, 34, 56
advertising agency of, 28
as helpmate, 27-28, 48
marriage to Steinbeck, 22
separation and divorce, 59-60

Steinbeck, Elaine Scott (third wife of Steinbeck), 7, 76, 99, 101
happy influence on Steinbeck, 84-87
marriage to Steinbeck, 79-80

Steinbeck, Elizabeth (sister of Steinbeck), 10

Steinbeck, Esther (sister of Steinbeck), 10

Steinbeck, Gwyndolyn Conger (second wife of Steinbeck), 68, 69
courtship and marriage to Steinbeck, 60-61
separation and divorce, 71-72, 75-76

Steinbeck, John
Arthurian theme and, 30-33, 89-91
communism and, 36
death of, 101
divorces
from Carol, 59-60
from Gwyndolyn, 75-76
ecological philosophy of, 66
education
Salinas High School, 13-14
Stanford University, 14-16
financial troubles of, 17-18, 27, 28, 88
Lake Tahoe, years at, 19-21
marine biology research, 55-57
marriages
to Carol, 22
to Elaine, 79-80
to Gwyndolyn, 60-61
Mexican research with Ricketts, 55-57
New York City
early and frustrating times in, 16-18
Nobel Prize, 7, 96-97
Pulitzer Prize, 58
serious illness, 91-93, 100-101

shyness of, 35, 52, 86
statements
    of self-appraisal, 39
    on author's privacy, 48
    on celebrity status, 44
    on convictions and ethics, 9
    on creative integrity, 51
    on doubt and resolution,
        32, 34, 74, 77
    on fame and typecasting, 35
    on fears, 19
    on hope for his future, 63
    on literature, 96-97
    on money, 88
    on moral erosion, 94, 97-98,
        100
    on motives for writing, 37
    on mystic event, 70
    on need for perfection, 78,
        80, 93
    on novel as art, 86
    on parenting, 76
    on personal growth, 21
    on political ideology, 37
    on rage of workers, 53
    on war, 59, 62, 63, 99
    on writer's inner wealth, 42
    on young writer's
        philosophy, 17
timeline of life, 6
variety of early jobs, 16-18
war correspondent
    Vietnam, 98-99
    World War II, 60-63
works of
    published
        *The Acts of King Arthur
            and His Noble Knights*,
            13, 90-91
        America and Americans, 98
        Bombs Away, 59
        Burning Bright, 77
        Cannery Row, 65-67
        Cup of Gold, 16, 19-21, 23
        East of Eden, 7, 10
        The Forgotten Village, 57-58
        The Grapes of Wrath, 7-9,
            48-55, 58
        "The Harvest Grapes,"
            45
        "I Go Back to Ireland," 85

In Dubious Battle, 8, 35-38
*Journal of a Novel: The
    "East of Eden" Letters*
    (posthumous), 82-83
*The Log from the "The Sea
    of Cortez,"* 57
The Moon is Down, 58-59
"The Murderer," 6
Of Mice and Men, 7, 8, 39-
    44
Once There Was a War, 62-
    63
The Pastures of Heaven,
    25-26
The Pearl, 67-68
"The Red Pony," 28-29
The Red Pony, 28-29
*The Short Reign of Pippin
    IV*, 89
"Starvation Under the
    Orange Trees," 47
Sweet Thursday, 87
To a God Unknown, 22-23
Tortilla Flat, 30-35
*Travels with Charley: In
    Search of America*, 95-98
The Wayward Bus, 68
*The Winter of Our
    Discontent*, 8, 94, 100
unpublished
    L'Affaire Lettuceburg, 47
    Dissonant Symphony, 22-23
Steinbeck, John Ernst (father of
    Steinbeck), 10-12, 26, 29-30, 35
Steinbeck, John (son of
    Steinbeck), 71, 76, 80-81, 94
Steinbeck, Mary (sister of
    Steinbeck), 10, 11, 90
Steinbeck, Olive Hamilton
    (mother of Steinbeck), 10-12,
    26, 29-30
Steinbeck, Thom (son of
    Steinbeck), 65, 69, 76, 80-81,
    94, 101
Steinbeck: A Life in Letters, 19, 25,
    32, 39, 42, 44, 48, 56, 61, 63,
    70, 73, 76, 78, 83, 86, 88, 95, 98
Stevenson, Adlai, 8
Street, Webster, 15, 19, 59-60, 63-
    65, 73, 80
Swedish Academy, 96

Sweet Thursday (Steinbeck), 87

Tarkington, Booth, 11
teleology, 41-42
The Time of Your Life (Saroyan),
    58
To a God Unknown (Steinbeck),
    22-23, 26-27
Tortilla Flat (Steinbeck), 30-35
    his first literary classic, 35
    movie version, 31, 38
Tracy, Spencer, 38
*Travels with Charley: In Search of
    America* (Steinbeck), 95-98
*The True Adventures of John
    Steinbeck, Writer* (Benson), 15,
    23, 35, 51
Twain, Mark, 101
Twentieth Century Fox Studios,
    56, 77

U.S. Foreign Information
    Service (FIS), 58

Viking Press, 48, 57, 89, 98
Vinaver, Eugene, 91
Viva Zapata! (movie), 77-79

Wagner, Edith, 30
Wagner, Jack, 70, 71, 79
Wagner, Max, 58, 60, 79
Wallsten, Mr. and Mrs. Robert,
    98
The Wayward Bus (Steinbeck),
    68, 72-73
Weedpatch (migrant camp), 43-
    44
Western Flyer (boat), 55-57
West, George, 43
Wilder, Thornton, 58
Wilhelmson, Carl, 14, 22, 25
Williams, Annie Laurie, 42, 70,
    77
The Winter of Our Discontent
    (Steinbeck), 8, 94, 100

Zanuck, Darryl F., 56, 77-78
Zapata, Emiliano, 70-71, 77-79

Picture Credits

About the Author

Tom Ito is a free-lance writer who resides in Los Angeles, California. His interest in the entertainment industry led him to publish *Yesteryears*, a magazine profiling television and radio celebrities, which he edited and distributed in the greater Los Angeles area from 1988 to 1990. Mr. Ito is the author of *Conversations with Michael Landon*, written in tribute to the late actor. He is working on his first novel.